GLORIOUS STENCILING

GLORIOUS STENCILING

Elaine Green

LAUREL
GLEN

Dedication
For my husband, Ian

A QUINTET BOOK

Published in the United States by
Laurel Glen Publishing,
An imprint of the Advantage Publishers Group
5880 Oberlin Drive, Suite 400
San Diego, CA 92121-4794
www.advantagebooksonline.com

All notations of errors or omissions should be addressed to
Laurel Glen Publishing, editorial department, at the above address.
All other correspondence (author inquiries, permissions and rights)
concerning the content of this book should be addressed to
Quintet Publishing Limited, 6 Blundell Street, London N7 9BH.

ISBN 1-57145-654-6

            Library of Congress Cataloging-in-Publication Data
Green, Elaine.
   Glorious stenciling / Elaine Green.
      p.cm.
   Includes bibliographical references and index.
   ISBN 1-57145-654-6
   1. Stencil work. I. Title.

TT270 .G74 1999
745.7'3--dc21
                                                    99-058176

This book was designed and produced by
Quintet Publishing Limited
6 Blundell Street
London N7 9BH

Creative Director: Richard Dewing
Art Director: Silke Braun
Designer: Steve West
Project Editor: Clare Hubbard
Editor: Anna Bennett
Photographer: Jonathan Russell Reed
Illustrator: Jennie Doodge

Typeset in Great Britain by
Central Southern Typesetters, Eastbourne
Manufactured in Singapore by Bright Arts Pte Ltd.
Printed in China by Leefung-Asco Printers Ltd.

Publisher's Note
When completing stenciling projects exercise care when using tools and
materials. Always follow the safety instructions given in this book, and always
read the manufacturer's instructions on packages and labels. Use paints
containing lead with care and when painting surfaces or items for children
it is essential to use lead-free, non-toxic paints. If using spray paints, always
wear goggles and a protective mask and work in a well-ventilated area.
To avoid inhaling the dust when sanding or sawing MDF a protective mask
should be worn.

CONTENTS

INTRODUCTION

Stenciling is an immensely popular and enjoyable way of decorating with unlimited creative potential. Applying a stencil is a technique that can easily be mastered by almost anyone, even those who claim to have no graphic skills at all, using materials that are readily available and relatively inexpensive, so that beginners need not feel daunted. Thanks to the availability of precut stencils in a wide range of interesting designs, professional results can be obtained with minimal effort. For those who prefer to design their own stencils, the possibilities are endless.

Although I have been stenciling for many years, the moment when the stencil is peeled back to reveal the image of a new design for the first time never fails to excite me. During recent years stenciling has moved on from the tentative borders used initially to far more adventurous finishes and effects. Once you have mastered the basic techniques, you can experiment with different finishes and effects: try stenciling using a tinted gloss varnish over a matt base to imitate damask-like patterns, for example, or building up richness by overlaying one stencil over another.

This book aims to teach you the basics by taking you through a variety of projects ranging from simple stenciling onto paper up to planning and decorating a whole room. You will discover some of the exciting ways in which stencils can be used either by making use of the stencils at the back of the book or by designing your own. I have included a number of different paints and techniques which are all quite simple to use and which I hope will lead you to further experiments. I have tried to show how you can achieve exciting results by thoughtful arrangement of the stencils themselves and careful consideration of the background on which they are to be placed. Detailed descriptions are given for each project and advice on finishes has also been included. The idea is for you to use from the projects described the steps you may wish to select for your own piece of work. The advance planning is half the fun. At each stage of your work you will be making decisions leading toward a completely individual and personal project. It has been a great pleasure to me that Caroline Brown has agreed to contribute three projects showing her lovely textiles together with a detailed description of the technique of spray painting, a method which produces unique and beautiful results. Caroline and I met more than twelve years ago while learning our stenciling skills from the master stenciler Lyn Le Grice. We had not met again until now and as we have both been stenciling continuously since then it has been fun catching up and exchanging ideas.

Stencils found on the walls of a fifteenth-century English house.

An age-old craft

Stenciling has been defined as "a drawing or printing plate with parts cut out to form a design that is to be copied onto a surface by laying the plate onto the surface and painting over the cut-out parts." The word itself is derived from the old French *estencillir*, which means to sparkle. Stenciling has been used as a method of decorating for many hundreds of years throughout the world, each country giving to the craft its own national characteristics. In England evidence of its use can be seen in churches dating from medieval times when it was frequently used as a background design on the decorated rood screens separating the nave from the choir, or to imitate the designs on rich fabrics worn by painted figures. Ancient stencil designs are still being discovered and preserved today, not only in churches but also in domestic dwellings that retain their original decorations. Sadly, over the years not everyone has recognized this work for what it is and a number of fine examples have been painted over. Today, with a greater interest in stencil decoration, owners of old houses are more likely to recognize early forms of this craft if they come across it and can contact the appropriate experts and have records taken before they start redecorating. Stenciling in England has been used continually as a way of decorating and the work of many famous names of the past such as Pugin, Burges, and Charles Rennie Mackintosh are still to be seen in all their colorful glory.

Stenciling is believed to have originated as an art form in China, possibly as early as 3000 BC. It spread to Japan where some examples of the work were so fine that the bridges linking the designs were made of human hair and virtually invisible. The Japanese also stenciled both sides when working on cloth so that the fabric looked as if it was woven. The countries of continental Europe have their own strong stenciling traditions, some of which found their way to colonial America where settlers used stencils as a way of decorating furniture, floors, and floorcloths. Examples have been found dating back to 1778.

You can see many examples of stenciling in museums, on items such as furniture, quilts, and rugs, which could be used as a starting point for the creation of your own designs.

As this is first and foremost a practical book, the background I have given is of necessity only a very brief introduction to the rich and varied story of stenciling. I have suggested some books for further reading at the end if you want to learn more. The advantage we have over our ancestors is the great diversity of convenient modern materials designed to make our work easier and quicker. There is greater attention to the safety aspect and as you will see in the following pages many products are now water-based and nontoxic and their quick-drying properties mean that we can avoid unpleasant fumes without compromising the quality of the finished work.

I very much hope you will find something in this book that catches your imagination and gives you the confidence to get started. Enjoy!

NOTE

In order to complete the projects, trace off the relevant stencil and cut it out before you begin work. Where a press-out stencil has been provided, this will be noted in the relevant project.

Wreath of Roses quilt
(78 in. square), American,
mid-nineteenth century.

American dower chest,
painted in Pennsylvania
Dutch style, c. 1785.

A stenciled floor in the American
Museum, Bath, England.

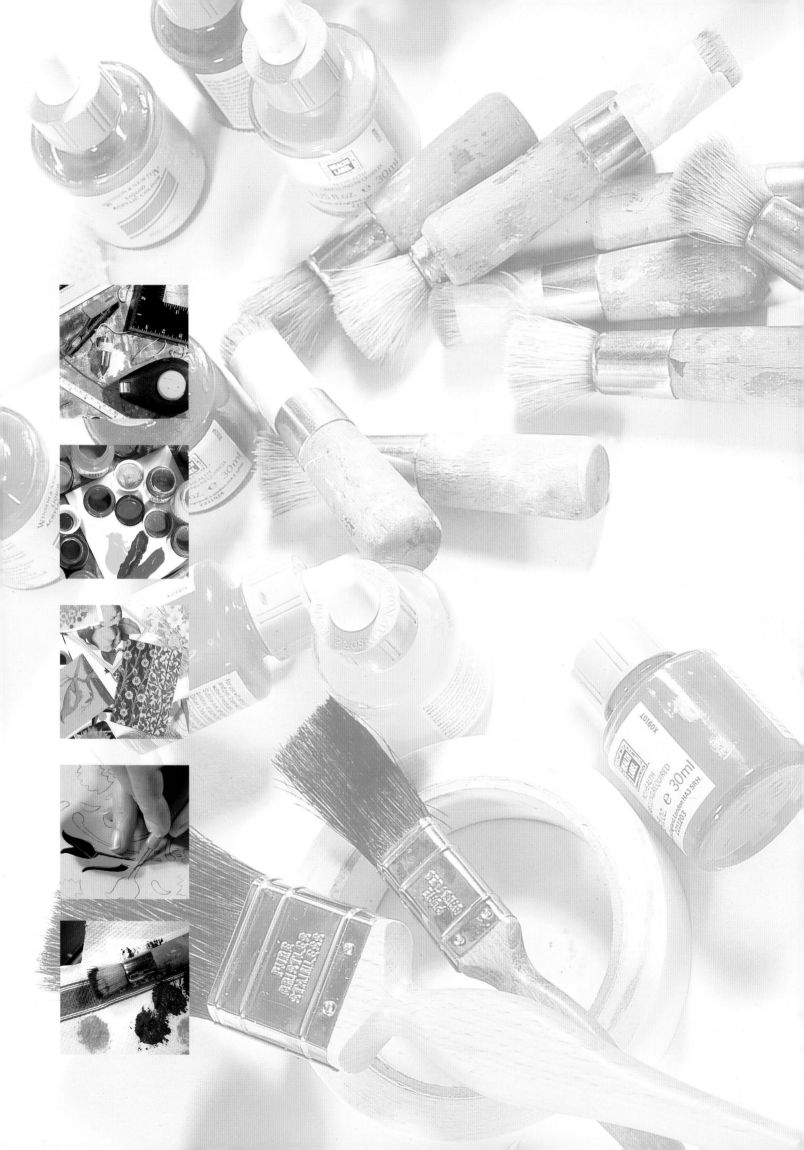

THE BASICS

A major advantage of decorating with stencils is that the tools and materials required need not be expensive. It is a craft where you can gradually build up your equipment as you need it, and if you are prepared to design and cut out your own stencils not only will you have the satisfaction of producing your own designs, but there is a considerable financial saving involved.

Be inventive with household materials such as kitchen sponges for applying paint, and try tying string around a foam roller so that the finished effect is mottled rather than flat. Keep empty yogurt pots to use as disposable containers for paint and varnish. Clean your brushes by rubbing the bristles across the rough surface of nylon pan cleaners. Save old tights for sieving lumpy paint and use old T-shirts for ragging on paints.

Remember that a simple design placed with imagination can be just as effective as something more complicated and ambitious.

Think about the space created around the stencil shape as much as the shape itself. Spend time trying out your ideas before you start. Having put time and effort into cutting out your stencil, try and get as much out of it as possible—see what it looks like upside down, flip it over to make a mirror image, try repeating it at regular intervals to make a border, and experiment with some of the different techniques described for applying paint. You will find suggestions to help you to organize your work in advance; time and effort spent measuring and working out where to place your design to the best advantage before you start will be well rewarded, even though you are longing to begin.

MATERIALS

Measuring equipment

Pair of compasses for drawing circles on geometric stencil patterns; dressmaker's measuring tape for use when working on fabrics; long metal retractable tape for general measuring and for walls; set square, especially useful when making floorcloths and checking corners; plumb line (a long piece of string with a weight on the end) to check that lines from floor to ceiling are vertical. (An improvised line can be made from a length of string with a key on the bottom; long nonslip metal rule, useful when working out border designs, measuring generally (especially floorcloths) and also for cutting straight lines on stencils); small spirit level, to check the level of borders around the top of a room where the ceiling line is uneven; large metal square for squaring off stencil card for large stencils and for checking corners accurately, especially when making floorcloths; chalk box, a box filled with chalk containing a long length of string (its use is described in detail in the floor-decorating project).

Masking tapes and glues

Two-sided tape for securing floorcloths to stop them slipping; ½-in.; and 1-in. masking tape, invaluable for stenciling, repairing stencils, masking areas, and so on. Do not leave tape on items longer than the manufacturer recommends: it can be very difficult to remove after a while and could remove the background on which you are working; red signwriter's low-tack tape, suitable for marking out lines. Adhesive, solvent-free craft glue used in floorcloth-making; fine line tape, a very fine low tack tape especially helpful for making thin lines on furniture (see the Writing Slope project page 53); stretch tape for marking out curved surfaces; low tack stencil tape; repositional nonpermanent adhesive; paper glue; 2½-in. low-tack decorator's tape, useful for masking round stencils, marking out stripes on walls and so on. In the center of the photograph is poster tack, useful for fixing stencils in position on surfaces where nonpermanent adhesive

would be unsuitable. A tube of border and repair adhesive (not shown) is useful when working on a wallpapered wall where the wallpaper is peeling off.

Stay-wet palette

Made by various artist's paint manufacturers, useful for keeping acrylic paints moist. The paints can be kept for some time once squeezed on to the surface, with the lid in place.

Equipment for applying paint

A sponge for creating background texture and for applying paints through the stencil plate; 2-in. sponge roller for stenciling larger shapes and for rolling on background paint. A miniroller, an alternative way of passing the paints through the stencil, covers very quickly and can make stenciling large areas of background much easier; you can then fill in the details with a brush. A roller can also have a different color at each end, which gives the design an interesting mottled look when passed through the stencil; a range of brushes in various sizes for painting in the background to be stenciled. The diagonal fitch is useful for awkward corners and areas where an accurate edge is needed; a commercially produced brush cleaner (the green square shown). Stencil brushes should always be washed out as soon as work is finished (acrylic paint is particularly difficult to remove if left on). Having washed out the brush in warm soapy water, rub it across the brush cleaner to remove any residual paint. An alternative is to rub the tips of the brush across a nylon scourer; the black roller tray is for use with sponge rollers. Put several teaspoons of paint into the well, run the roller across this, then even out the paint by running the roller across the ridged top of the tray; in the center is a range of stencil brushes of different sizes, the large ones for stencils with large coverage such as floors and very small ones for detailed work.

Always buy the very best stencil brushes you can afford. For each new stenciling job you will need a separate brush for each color group. It is worth taking good care of your brushes and storing them properly (bristles upward) so that bristles do not become damaged. Always make sure that you have a set of clean and dry brushes for each job.

Papers and stencil card

Cartridge paper for working out design ideas; acetate for making stencils; carbon paper, useful for transferring a design onto stencil cards (should not be used to transfer a design onto the object to be decorated as the marks are difficult to remove); graphite paper for transferring marks directly onto the object to be decorated; tracing paper for tracing designs; decorator's lining paper, an inexpensive but useful paper for testing out designs, masking out areas and so on; oiled Manila stencil card for making stencils; on top of the Manila card is a second type of acetate for making stencils. A number of different types are available, but the best are those with a rough side on which you can draw; in the center, graph paper for working out regular and geometric patterns. Not shown, but useful, is overhead projector film suitable for photocopiers (available from office suppliers)—the design can be photocopied directly onto this.

PAINTS

Most paints are suitable for stenciling so long as they dry quickly and are of a creamy consistency so that they will not run under the stencils. There are a number of paints produced especially for stenciling but I prefer the freedom of mixing my own colors and I usually use acrylic tube paints. It is preferable to buy artist's quality colors where possible; not only are the colors better, but they also have a higher degree of permanence.

NOTE It is always important when using new products to read the manufacturers' instructions carefully and to act on their advice for the best results.

Acrylic paints

They are water-soluble, flow well, and come in a wide range of colors. As they dry very quickly it can sometimes help to mix in a small amount of acrylic retardant to delay the drying time. Brushes should be washed in warm soapy water immediately after use, as the paint is very difficult to remove if it is allowed to harden on the brush. Liquid acrylic paints are also available, which are dispensed with a dropper and are very convenient to use.

Emulsion or latex

Many decorating stores sell sample pots as testers. These are an ideal size for stencil painting. The solvent is water and brushes should be washed out as soon as you have finished. These paints are also very suitable for covering large areas and work well with minirollers or 2-in. rollers for speed.

Spray paints

These paints are particularly suitable for painting onto surfaces such as enameled fridge doors, glass windows, and most other surfaces with the exception of ceramic tiles. The big advantage is that there is no equipment to clean. The use of spray paint is described in detail on pages 24–25. They do require a little practice but, with patience, you will eventually achieve rewarding results. The solvent for these if you are using them on hard surfaces is acetone or a small amount of cellulose thinners. Be careful with the latter as they can remove the background paint as well.

Signwriter's enamels

These paints give a good, luminous coverage. They work well for stenciling onto all surfaces and can be used on glass and stove enamel such as refrigerators. Some produce a translucent effect similar to stained glass. The solvent is mineral spirit. Because some of these paints contain lead they are not suitable for children's furniture or toys.

Japan paints

These have good colors and are quick-drying but are not available everywhere. The solvent is mineral spirit.

GIFTWRAP

A gift can be made more special by using hand-decorated giftwrap. Ordinary brown wrapping paper can lend itself to a number of decorative possibilities. Gold stenciling across the faintly striped brown of the paper can be very effective, particularly for Christmas gifts; tie the gift with gold ribbon, or try colored raffia for a stylish and elegant effect. By decorating your own giftwrap you can incorporate specific, highly personal motifs which relate to the occasion or the interests of the recipient. In this project by first coloring and then stenciling the paper you can produce something that is both original and personal.

YOU WILL NEED

- brown wrapping paper
- $1\frac{1}{2}$-in. paint brush
- large wooden board
- gummed paper strip
- acrylic paints: monestial blue, monestial green, and gold
- white tile
- cloth
- bronze powder
- repositional adhesive
- stencils (press-out supplied)
- 2 stencil brushes
- paper towels
- wide ribbon—choose a color that will co-ordinate with the giftwrap—I have used golden yellow here
- ruler
- pencil
- blank card suitable for decorating (e.g. a small sheet of cartridge paper, folded)
- hole punch
- thin ribbon that will coordinate with the card—golden yellow was used here

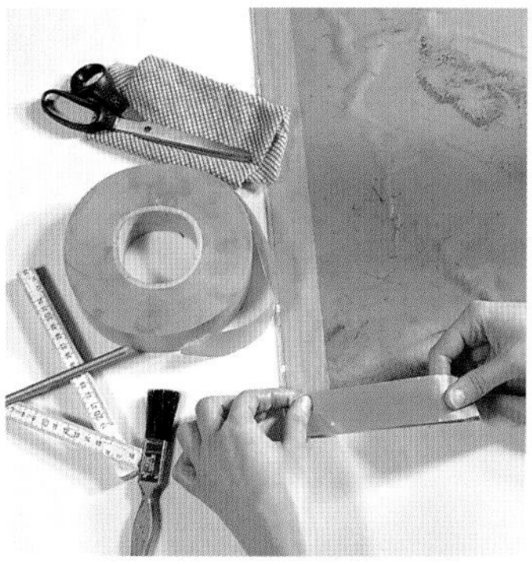

ONE

To get the paper to lie flat, wet the paper on both sides, lay onto the wooden board allowing a margin of wooden board all round the paper, gently smooth into place, and tape around the edges with the gummed paper strip.

TWO

Leave to dry. Check that it has dried smooth and taut. Leave the gummed paper in place until you have completed the stenciling.

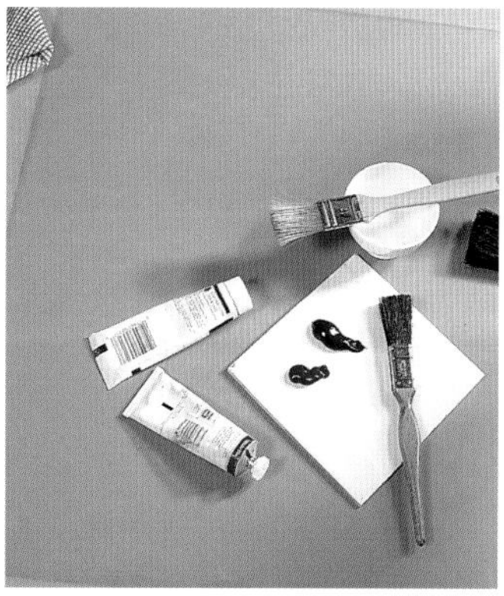

TECHNIQUES USED

- stretching paper for painting
- registering and stenciling a half-drop pattern
- simple ragging
- shadowing

THREE

Squeeze about $1\frac{1}{4}$ in. monestial blue acrylic paint onto the white tile and using plenty of water quickly paint all over the paper, dabbing with a cloth as you go. Then squeeze out about $1\frac{1}{4}$ in. monestial green and work this into the damp background, again dabbing with the cloth to soften the marks and to allow the blue to show through here and there. Do not worry if the paper appears to swell and wrinkle again as it will become flat as it dries. Leave to dry overnight.

FOUR

To stencil the all-over pattern squeeze about 1¼ in. gold acrylic paint onto a clean white tile and add a little bronze powder for added sparkle. Working from the top left-hand side, lay the stencil down—you cannot use tape to fix the stencil as you will tear the paper but instead use nonpermanent repositional glue on the back. Mix together the bronze powder and gold paints with a brush and take up the mixture onto the end of a clean stencil brush. Work off the excess onto the paper towels and paint through the stencil. Make sure you stencil in the registration mark to the right, which will help you with the positioning, when you come to the next row across.

SIX

The same stencil is used to decorate the ribbon with the shapes at the sides blanked out to make the design fit the ribbon. In the press-outs at the back of the book you will find that this has already been done for you. Measure the width of the ribbon and make a mark each side of the stencil the same width as the ribbon.

FIVE

Continue down the row placing the little heart shape at the top of the stencil over the little heart shape at the bottom of the newly painted stencil. Work your way down to the bottom of the paper in this way using the little heart shape as registration. For the next row position the stencil so that the leaf registration to the left covers the leaf mark which you made to the right of the design as you worked the first row. This should form a half-drop repeat pattern, so that as you work across the paper you will see that four large hearts form a diamond shape.

SEVEN

Squeeze a little blue and green paint onto the tile repeating the method used for the giftwrap. Match the top small heart to the bottom small heart on the previous shape as you work down, making sure that the pencil marks on the stencil are in line with the sides of the ribbon.

EIGHT

To make a greetings card to match, stencil a heart onto the front of the blank card lightly in green just below the center point and slightly to the right.

NINE

Slide the stencil up and to the left and paint over part of the original shape in blue. This technique is called shadowing and can be used to give a three-dimensional effect. Punch holes in the card and tie with thin gold ribbon.

VARIATION

Stars make an excellent motif. Try decorating the parcel with a contrasting colored ribbon, also decorated with stars.

LAMPSHADE

Decorated paper lampshades are very attractive and quick to make. With the help of a special brass fitting to support them they can be cut to any size and may be stenciled with a design to suit a particular theme—Christmas, a birthday, a romantic Valentine's dinner, or an anniversary. Shades for bedside lamps can be decorated to blend in with the soft furnishings, perhaps taking a single flower from a floral pattern on the drapes and turning it into a stencil. The possibilities are infinite. The template shown here allows the bottom edge to be straight or scalloped. It is important when your work is finished to use a fire-retardant spray and do not allow the light bulb to come into contact with the paper shade.

YOU WILL NEED

- stiff card 250 gms weight in the color of your choice (cream is used here)
- pencil
- stencil (template page 123)
- nonpermanent glue
- designer's liquid acrylic paints used here (ultramarine blue, bright yellow, bright red, white, monestial blue, lemon yellow) but most acrylic paints would be suitable
- white tile
- 4 stencil brushes
- paper towels
- scissors
- PVA glue
- 2 paper clips
- fire-retardant spray
- brass fitting for electric light
- light stand

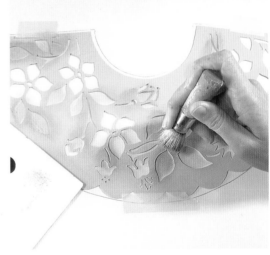

ONE
Draw round the template onto the card. The template is a little larger than the stencil given to allow a narrow margin at the top, which will be stenciled as a fine borderline as shown.

TWO
Run the nonpermanent glue around the edge of the back of the stencil. Fix the stencil in position over the traced outline, allowing for the small margin at the top as described. Squeeze a little ultramarine blue and bright yellow paint onto the white tile. Mix these for the leaves and stalks. Take up the paint onto the tip of the stencil brush and wipe off the excess on the paper towels. Stencil all the leaves and the stalks.

THREE

Leave the stencil in place and mix together bright red, bright yellow, and white on a clean part of the tile. Add the red and yellow to the white, not the other way round. When you have achieved a soft apricot color, take up the paint with a clean stencil brush and, having wiped off the excess paint on paper towels, stencil in all the flowers using a circular movement with your brush. Stencil the tips of any buds as well. Now dip your brush lightly into the bright red. Do not do this too enthusiastically, as you do not want the color to be too bright. Wipe off the excess on paper towels and stipple the center of each flower only.

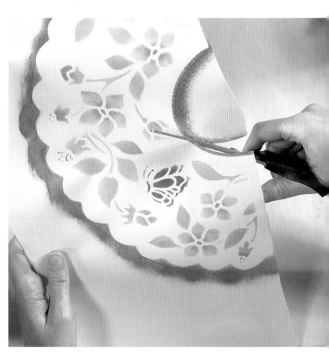

FOUR

Still leaving the stencil in place stencil the butterfly. Starting with the white paint, add a little lemon yellow and very gradually a little monestial blue—this should make a delicate blue-green. Using the third brush stencil the butterfly with this mix, and finally add a very little of just the monestial blue onto the same brush and use this to define the edges of the butterfly's wings. Stencil the scallops up to the edge of the template and the margin at the top with this color as well.

FIVE

Making sure the paint is dry, cut out the shape.

SIX

Paste a thin line of glue down the seam and position the other end of the shade over this. While the glue is drying keep the seam in position with a paper clip fixed at the top and bottom. Finally spray over the whole shade with fire-retardant spray.

VARIATION

The lampshade can be decorated to coordinate with any room, or any occasion. This lamp could be part of a decorative Christmas table.

CHRISTMAS
tablecloth

I have used a paper cloth for this stenciling project but if you wish to make something a little more permanent, a large white sheet would be suitable. The procedure is the same but fabric paints would need to be used. The important thing is to measure the piece of paper or cloth in order to put the stencils in the right place. Although a cloth decorated for a Christmas meal is shown, there is a whole host of occasions when a decorated cloth would be appropriate, including weddings, birthdays, and anniversaries. The galleon design could be used on a child's toy or, evenly spaced, on ceramic tiles in a bathroom. The holly wreaths could be stenciled onto a window or door panel during the festive season. The holly can be used on napkins to match the tablecloth, round a Christmas apron or on giftwrap. A word of warning—as you are working on a large area make sure you keep all your painting equipment on a separate small table and, to avoid spillages, do not succumb to the temptation to place them on top of your work while decorating.

YOU WILL NEED

- a white paper tablecloth or sheet
- tailor's chalk
- a pair of compasses
- stencil (templates pages 124–25 and press-outs supplied)
- extra card to use for template and marker
- repositional nonpermanent adhesive
- acrylic paint in copper/gold, dark green, and bright red
- 3 stencil brushes
- paper towels
- white tile
- thumbtack
- tape measure

ONE

Find the center of the tablecloth and mark it lightly with the tailor's chalk. If you are using a sheet, fold it in half then iron a crease along the fold and repeat the other way. Where the creases bisect is the center. Lay the cloth out flat on a large, clean flat surface.

TWO

The design of this cloth illustrates the Christmas carol *I Saw Three Ships*. As an alternative, a Christmas bell can replace the galleons. The galleon is designed to decorate the center of the cloth and in order to fit in the three ships a circle with a radius of 3½ in. is drawn with the compasses on a template.

The center of the circle matches the center of the tablecloth. The circle is divided equally into three points and the bottom of these points shows where the ships are to go. Cover the back of the stencil with repositional adhesive (do not use tape, because it would tear the paper).

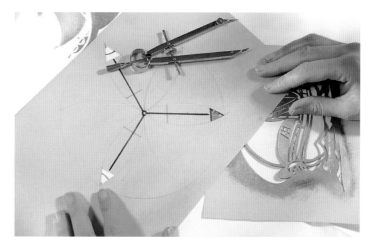

THREE

Shake the pot of gold paint, unscrew the lid, and dip the stencil brush into the lid of the pot, wiping off the excess on paper towels. Using a circular motion stencil the entire ship except for the flag.

FOUR

Drop a few drops of bright red paint onto the white tile and with the second brush stencil in the flag. Remove the stencil, leaving the template in place, and position the ship stencil under the second point on the circle. Stencil this in the same way and when this is complete move to the third point and stencil the third ship. With the gold paint and the star stencil decorate around the base of the ships.

FIVE

Next decorate the holly circle. The holly stencil forms exactly half a circle and there is a dot to show the center. Measure how far the center of this circle is to go from the center of the cloth. Make a note of this measurement so that all the other circles are stenciled the same distance from the center. Use a point between the two ships for guidance as shown on the template. The position of the other three circles is worked out just below the ships. Place a thumbtack through the point marking the center of the stencil. Using the third brush and dark green paint, paint in the top half of the holly wreath, stencil the leaves dark green and the berries bright red. When this has been completed, pivot the stencil round keeping the thumbtack in place and stencil the bottom half. A total of six circles are worked in this way.

Using the holly and ribbon stencils work out where the corner pieces are to go, stencil the holly in dark green, the berries and the ribbon in red. You can also center sprigs of holly and ribbon around the cloth, 2 in. from the edge. Sprinkle the corners with stars.

SIX

Because the wording of the carol is to be repeated it is better to cut out the whole sentence onto stencil card so that the spacing can be adjusted on the stencil card. It would be very difficult to make alterations on the tablecloth. On the stencil card draw a line across the base about ½ in. from the edge. Using this as a guide and using the alphabet stencils, stencil the message across the strip. Decide how far from the edge the message is to go and make a template to attach to the base which exactly comes to the edge of the tablecloth. Using the crease marking the center of each side, center the wording and position the stencil. Stencil the letters in bright red.

TECHNIQUES USED

* ❋ stenciling a paper tablecloth
* ❋ working out measurements
* ❋ finding the center
* ❋ using a stencil alphabet

WOOD

Stenciling looks effective against the natural grain of pine. Water-based wood stains can also be used cleverly to suggest marquetry, and small sample pots of different colors of wood stain can be bought, which would be eminently suitable for stenciling.

Plain white can look stark because the bridges of the stencil already break up the designs, so soften the background with sponging.

Small wooden objects such as wastebaskets, picture frames, small sets of shelves, and so on, now often made in medium-density fiberboard (MDF), are easy to decorate quickly and effectively, and require little of the tiring preparation work required for similar pieces made in wood as they have a smooth surface and no knots. MDF has certainly revolutionized decorative painting from this point of view but a slight disadvantage of this material is that it is not always as resistant to knocks as wood and will bruise if treated roughly. If sawing or sanding MDF always wear a protective mask to avoid inhaling the fine dust. To make life easier when decorating I usually suggest removing lids, doors, drawers, and so on, where possible, taking care not to let paint build up too thickly along the edges of these, as they will not shut properly when replaced if this happens.

It is possible that the piece you are about to work on has already been painted, so all that is needed is a wipe with a damp cloth and a little detergent so that it will accept the stencil paint. When working on small objects it is best to leave a space around your design so the final effect is not too cramped, and to try and keep your design in scale with the piece you are working on.

PICTURE
frame

Choosing the right frame can greatly enhance the picture it is to contain. Photographs, paintings, certificates, and even favorite postcards can all look far more impressive if some thought is given to their framing. Mirrors, too, can look dramatic with a decorative border. Attractive frames can be expensive to buy but many stores stock a large variety of relatively cheap wooden frames which are suitable for decoration.

You can also make your own frame to the size and shape you want by using a mitering device. For this project a square piece of ½-in. thick MDF was used, from which a square was cut out from the center appropriate to the size of the picture. When cutting or sanding MDF you should always wear a mask. A narrow molding around the outer and inner edges was attached to this—the inner molding also formed the rebate to hold the picture.

YOU WILL NEED

- wood filler
- sandpaper
- red oxide colored emulsion paint
- 1-in. paint brush
- candle
- matt black emulsion paint
- fine wire wool
- a piece of paper
- white chalk
- ballpoint pen
- low-tack masking tape
- stencils (press-outs provided)
- gold varnish
- stencil brush
- mineral spirit
- gold wax
- dead-flat acrylic varnish

TWO
Rub over raised areas of molding with the candle to act as a resist for the next layer of paint. Don't do this too vigorously, as the finished effect should be subtle.

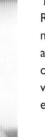

ONE
Fill in any nail marks or cracks with wood filler and allow to dry. Wearing a protective mask, sand down. Paint the whole of the frame with red oxide colored emulsion and allow to dry.

THREE
Paint over the whole frame with matt black emulsion and allow to dry. Rub over the raised sections of the molding with fine wire wool. The paint over the areas rubbed with the candle will come away revealing the red paint underneath.

SIX

Dip your finger into the gold wax and rub round the inner and outer edgings of the moldings. To protect your work, finish with a coat of dead-flat acrylic varnish.

FOUR

To stencil, first find the center of each side. Cut a piece of paper the exact length and width of the flat surface of the long and short sides. Fold this in half lengthwise and open out. Rub the chalk over the back of the paper. Lay the long strip of paper over the corresponding side of the frame and draw over the fold with a ballpoint pen, and the chalk backing will make a mark on the frame showing where the center is. Using the shorter piece of paper, repeat the process with the short side of the frame. Mark all four sides in this way.

FIVE

Using the low tack tape to position the stencil, first stencil each corner using the corner stencil and the gold varnish. Shake the varnish bottle well and when you remove the lid you can dip your brush into the varnish which remains in the lid. Any corrections can be made with mineral spirit. When all the corners have been completed start with the first long side. Taking the border stencil, place the daisy center over the chalk mark and stencil up to the corner having first covered the corner with a small piece of card. Turn the stencil over, and stencil up to the second corner. Repeat for all four sides.

GARDEN
basket

This trug has a prettily shaped handle and when bought it was in bare pine. As a contrast to working with medium-density fiberboard which has a perfectly smooth surface I wanted to retain the "woody" look of this item, which I felt would be an appropriate background to the rustic theme with which I planned to stencil it. I first soaked the basket in a bowl of water to raise the grain of the wood and then allowed it to dry. I then prepared it by filling in any nail holes with wood filler, sanding down any rough edges caused through the original sawing but leaving any small imperfections in the wood itself. The whole basket was then sealed with a coat of sanding sealer and any knots in the pine sealed with knotting to avoid resin leaking from them with the passage of time.

YOU WILL NEED

- sample pot bright blue emulsion, latex or traditional paint, 8 fl. oz.
- sample pot egg-yolk yellow emulsion, latex or traditional paint, 8 fl. oz.
- dead-flat acrylic varnish
- stencils (templates page 126 and press-out supplied)
- acrylic paints ("golden" acrylic paints which are particularly suitable for stenciling were used) in white, yellow, burnt umber, black, dark green, bright red, and gray
- low tack tape
- 4 stencil brushes
- 1¼-in. paint brush
- white tile
- fine artist's brush
- lining paper

TWO
Reverse the stencil and decorate underneath the handle working out your design as you go along. When this is complete, using the artist's brush, fill in the center of the flowers with bright yellow paint.

ONE
Paint two coats of blue on the outside of the basket. When this is dry paint the inside with bright yellow. When the paint is completely dry, cover all painted surfaces with the dead-flat acrylic varnish. To decorate the handle I have used part of the stencil for the Giftwrap project (see press-outs). Position the stencil with the low tack tape. Stencil the daisy shapes in bright red and the leaves in dark green, leaving the stencil in place as you work.

THREE
Decide where the various elements given on the goose stencil sheet in the back of the book will be placed. I have used the corn each end of the sides. Stencil this in bright yellow and then lightly dip your stencil brush in burnt umber and stencil the base of the corn with this. Reverse the stencil and place it at the other end of the side.

FOUR

Decide where the first goose is to be placed. Position the stencil with low tack tape. Stencil the whole shape in white first, lifting the wing flap, which has been attached with tape at the top of the goose.

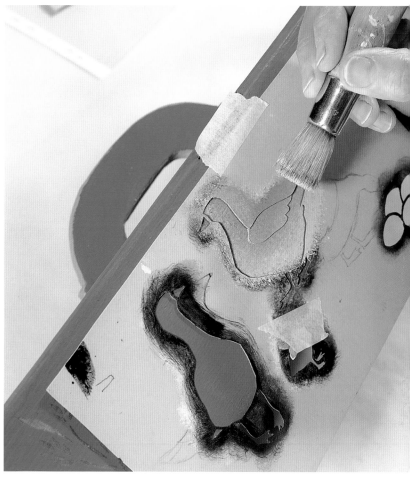

FIVE

Lay the wing flap down onto the goose and stencil over this with the gray color, using a stippling motion. Leaving the stencil in place, and using the brush with yellow paint, stencil in the beak and feet. When this has been finished, lift off the stencil and mark the eye with a black dot using the fine artist's brush. Continue in this way to stencil in any other geese. The goslings will work the same way using yellow instead of white for their bodies.

TECHNIQUES USED

* preparation of bare pine for stenciling
* making up a scene using several stencils
* stenciling in birds' wings
* variation on the original stencil for the Giftwrap project (see page 33)

VARIATION

The stencils can be enlarged and used as a template for embroidery, first stretching the embroidery canvas onto a board and using a single-color fabric paint which is heat-sealed to prevent the paint leaking onto the embroidery thread. This would make a nice theme for a child's cotton bib or apron.

SIX

Using the stencil brush with dark green paint and the grass stencil, stencil in a horizon at the back, taking care not to overlap the geese already painted. Finish with a coat of varnish. You can vary the scene shown using the various elements provided. If you are unsure as to what the end result will look like, experiment first on lining paper.

TRAY

Trays lend themselves to a whole range of decorative styles—rustic for garden use, stylish for entertaining, fresh and cheerful for breakfast. The possibilities are endless. Ready-made trays are easily found, often with a white heatproof plastic covered base and a wooden surround, so this is a typical example for decoration.

YOU WILL NEED

- stiff metal brush
- coarse sandpaper
- PVA to paint over the heatproof surface
- fine wire wool
- liming wax
- soft cloth
- clear wax
- latex or emulsion paint (bright blue for the background, bright yellow for the sunflowers, pale yellow and leaf green for the leaves
- water-based dead-flat acrylic varnish
- stencils (templates page 126 and press-outs supplied)
- lining paper
- 5 stencil brushes
- white tile
- acrylic paint in burnt sienna and burnt umber for the center of the sunflowers. Bright black and red for the ladybug
- brush for mixing
- small piece of bubble wrap
- water-based floor-quality varnish
- low-tack masking tape

ONE

Using the stiff metal brush, brush briskly over the pine surround of the tray to open up the grain. Sand down the white base to provide a key for the paint. Give the base a coat of PVA. With the fine wire wool work the liming wax into the pine. Allow 5 minutes to dry then remove the excess with a soft cloth. Finally, apply a coat of clear wax. Paint the base of the tray bright blue. Allow to dry and if necessary apply a second coat of paint. When this is dry paint over a light coat of acrylic varnish.

TWO

Plan where you are going to place your sunflower heads. At this stage you might wish to practice stenciling sunflower heads on the lining paper until you are satisfied with the result. Allowing for the petals round the center, place the cut-out circle where the center of the flower is to be and cover it with tape.

THREE

Stencil the petals with the stencil brush using a circular motion. First use the bright yellow and work your way around the circle, overlapping the petals as you go and making sure the base of the petals always comes over the edge of the center circle.

FOUR

When the petals form a circle, go round once more with the pale yellow. Do not attempt to cover the previous petals but always make sure the base comes a little over the center circle.

FIVE

To stencil the center of the flowers remove the card circle and place the card with the circle cut out over the space left in the center of the petals. On the tile mix together burnt sienna and burnt umber acrylic paint to make a rich brown. Add a little water to thin the mix. Paint the circle keeping a fraction away from the edge to keep the paint from creeping underneath.

SIX

Quickly lay the bubble wrap over the wet paint bubble-side down and press down firmly. When it is pulled away it should leave a clear imprint. Leave to dry. Work the other sunflower heads in the same way. Leave to dry.

SEVEN

Taking the leaf stencil, position the leaf in the spaces around the sunflowers and stencil with the green paint, using a stippling motion stipple up to the edge of the petals, checking through the stencil as you go that you do not stencil over the petals.

EIGHT

Decide where you want the ladybug to be before you stencil it. Because this is a whole shape with no bridges it can be placed on the flowers over your previous stenciling if you wish. Using the whole shape and bright red acrylic paint stipple over this. Remove the stencil and place the stencil with the dots and legs over the red shape. Using the black paint stipple in the dots and the legs. When all your work is quite dry paint over the whole of the base with at least three coats of floor-quality water-based acrylic varnish, allowing two hours between each coat. This will make the tray tough and heatproof. If you do not want a glossy finish add a final coat of deaf-flat acrylic varnish.

PORTABLE
writing desk

A small, portable writing desk is an ideal object for decoration. It is very useful to have somewhere to store writing paper, stamps, postcards etc. all in one place. This one is made of medium-density fiberboard ready for decorating which reduces the amount of preparation work, because the surface is already smooth. This is quite a small item so I painted the inside as well, finishing it off with the owner's initials inside. As the box is to be decorated inside and out, remove the lid to make it easier to paint. Keep the hinges and screws in a labeled tin. Seal all surfaces with sanding sealer.

YOU WILL NEED

- sample pot old rose pink emulsion or latex paint, 8 fl. oz.
- 1¼-in. paint brush
- fine line tape ⅛ in. wide
- sample pot blue-gray emulsion or latex paint, 8 fl. oz.
- cotton buds
- dead-flat acrylic varnish
- stencil (template page 127 and press-outs supplied)
- lining paper
- low-tack masking tape
- acrylic paints in titanium white, raw umber, cadmium red, yellow ocher, and ultramarine blue
- brush for mixing
- white tile
- 4 stencil brushes
- fine artist's brush
- dark oak furniture wax
- cotton wool
- soft cloth
- mineral spirit

ONE

Paint the base and lid inside and out with the pink emulsion. Allow to dry. If necessary apply a second coat and allow to dry.

TWO

Using the fine line tape, run the tape about ½ in. away from the edge all round the lid of the box and make sure it is smoothed down. Tape round the outside of the base, crossing the tapes over in the front center. It is a matter of preference where you would like the lining to be. It is there to define the shape of the box and to contain the stencil design.

THREE

With the blue-gray emulsion, paint over the outside of the lid and the outside of the base, painting over the fine line tape and leaving the inside of the box and the molding pink. Leave to dry.

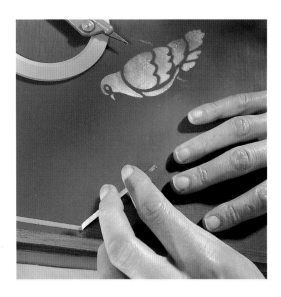

FOUR

Remove the fine line tape and tidy any paint that has crept underneath with a damp cotton bud. Paint a coat of dead-flat acrylic varnish over the outside of the lid and base. Decide where the doves and the blossom are to be stenciled. Using the stencils designed for this project try out some arrangements on a piece of lining paper first. Then position the stencil for the birds using low-tack tape. Stencil in titanium white first. Without removing the stencil make a mix using a little raw umber with titanium white and a very little blue to make a stone color.

FIVE

Using the stone color define the shape of the doves by working the stencil brush around the edges of the birds. With a clean brush stencil the beaks with yellow ocher. When the stencil is removed fill in the eyes with a dark mix of ultramarine blue and raw umber with a fine artist's brush. To stencil the blossom, mix some titanium white and a small amount of cadmium red and yellow ocher on the tile adding the last two colors to the titanium white until you obtain a soft peach color. Mix together the ultramarine blue and yellow ocher for the leaves on another part of the tile. Stencil in the blossom and leaves, using separate brushes for the peach and green. As you have varnished after painting the base coat, you should be able to wipe off any errors immediately with a little liquid detergent on a damp cloth without disturbing the base.

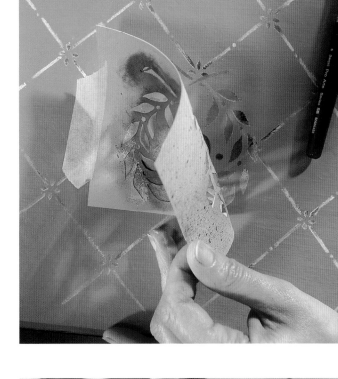

TECHNIQUES USED

❋ lining using masking tape
❋ color mixing
❋ antiquing using dark wax
❋ using stencils to create a small scene

SEVEN

If you wish to stencil the inside of the lid, do it now. You may wish to add initials or a small motif. I chose a decorative pattern with a central motif. Varnish with dead-flat acrylic varnish. Replace the lid and screw the hinges back into position.

SIX

Continue adding leaves and blossoms until you are satisfied with your arrangement. Stencil in the butterfly using the ultramarine blue mixed with a little titanium white. When all the paint has dried coat with dark oak furniture wax to give a mellow antique look to your work. If this appears too dark, tone down with a little mineral spirit on a ball of cotton wool. Buff to a shine with a soft cloth.

CERAMICS & GLASS

China responds well to stenciling, but as the surface is slippery it is easier to begin with flat surfaces such as large plates, graduating to more complicated shapes as you gain in practice. Some types of acetate stencils are easier to bend round curved surfaces and it is best to keep the shape simple and not try too much detail. It is a good idea to choose a theme for your china that complements other items. Once heat-cured, decorated china should be dishwasher-safe. A stenciled tile table-top for the garden is another useful idea.

Some lovely effects can be achieved by stenciling onto windows, as a pleasant way of providing a screen and as an alternative to frosted glass.

It is important to ensure that the surface is thoroughly clean and free of grease before stenciling, to allow sufficient time for the paint to cure, and to avoid decorating glass in an area which is subjected to constant damp because this gives rise to condensation; although this can be partially overcome by double glazing after decorating, the paint can eventually slide off. Proprietary window cleaning products can damage your work so when cleaning wipe over with a damp cloth only to protect the paint.

Glass paints for stenciling have many possibilities and, as alterations are made so easily, they are fun to experiment with. Allow at least a week for your paints to cure when you have finished your work. It can be cleaned with a little liquid detergent on a soft cloth after that.

CERAMIC
jug

The simple ladybug and leaf stencils used here are intended to complement the Tray project (see page 49). Until fairly recently paint used for painting china was spirit-based to make it adhere well to the china but water-based paints are now available which are less hazardous, more convenient, and also quick-drying. You can cure the paints to enamel hardness by baking the finished work in a domestic oven. Brushes can be washed out in water and a little liquid detergent and any corrections necessary can easily be made by wiping off with a damp cotton bud. Once baked your work becomes dishwasher-safe and resistant to wear.

YOU WILL NEED

- latex gloves
- mineral spirit or denatured alcohol
- cotton wool
- stencils (template page 126 and press-outs supplied)
- low-tack masking tape
- cocktail sticks
- white tile
- water-based ceramic paints in bright red and leaf green (Pebeo Porcelaine 150)
- 3 stencil brushes
- paper towels
- relief outliner in anthracite. (This comes in a tube which makes it possible to draw with the paint)

ONE
Wearing protective latex gloves, clean and degrease all surfaces to be decorated with mineral spirit or denatured alcohol on cotton wool. This will help the paint to stick to the slippery surface.

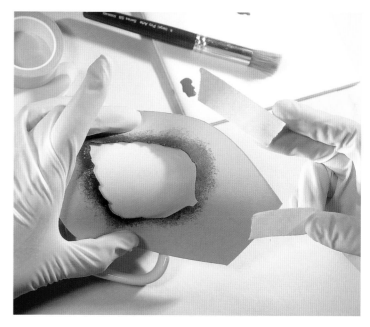

TWO
Position the leaf stencil where you want it to be, using low-tack masking tape. With a cocktail stick decant a few drops of the green paint onto the white tile just before you are ready to use it as the paint dries quickly. Take up the paint onto the tip of your stencil brush. Remove surplus paint onto a paper towel and stencil the leaf using a stippling motion. Just before the paint is dry use the tip of a cocktail stick to mark out the veins. Allow the paint to dry for 10 minutes as the ladybug is going to overlap the leaf and you do not wish to disturb the first coat of green paint.

THREE

Following the same procedure, fix the ladybug base stencil in position overlapping the leaf and decant a few drops of the red paint onto the tile. With a clean stencil brush stencil the ladybug in red and remove the stencil. Leave to dry.

FOUR

Squeeze a small amount of relief outliner onto the tile. Fix the spot stencil over the red base of the ladybug and with the third brush stencil in the spots. Remove the stencil. Because the stencil is so small and the surface slippery it is easier to draw in the legs free-hand with the relief outliner. You can practice with the outliner on the tile beforehand until you feel you are able to control the flow. Finally leave your work to air-dry for 24 hours then place in a slow oven. Set the oven to 300°F and when the required heat has been reached set a timer for 35 minutes. When baked turn off the oven and leave your work to cool.

VARIATION

Ceramic tiles can be successfully stenciled to create interesting and unusual decorative effects. The farm animals and checkerboard designs shown here would work well in a child's room.

CANDLE *holder*

Although the principles of stenciling on glass are similar to those of working on ceramics the difference is that while ceramics are opaque, glass is translucent, which makes for interesting decisions as to how you are going to decorate it. The technique I have used here is worked onto a glass candle holder, which can make a dramatic addition to a dining table or to light a dark corner. Take care never to leave a lit candle unattended.

YOU WILL NEED

- mineral spirit
- a soft lint-free rag
- stencil (press-out supplied)
- cocktail sticks
- colored cold-cure glass paints of your choice
- white tile
- stencil brushes, one for each color
- cerne outliner in silver and/or gold
- cotton buds
- crystal thixotropic (gold iridescent)
- round-ended kitchen knife or spatula (I used a plastic disposable knife)

ONE

Make sure the item you are decorating is absolutely clean and free of smears; wash it first with warm soapy water if necessary. Degrease the surface with mineral spirit on a lint-free rag to help the paint to adhere. If you are decorating the storm lamp as illustrated here, you might find it easier to slip it over a paper towel holder so you can have both hands free. Using the star stencil, stencil over the surface of the glass. You will need to hold the stencil in place by hand as tape would mark the glass. With a clean cocktail stick, decant a few drops of colored glass paint on to the tile, taking this up with your stencil brush, remove surplus paint and stencil the stars with a stippling motion. This paint dries very quickly.

TWO

Continue over the surface of the piece you are decorating, working out the balance of the design as you go. You can easily make alterations at this stage by wiping the paint off with a damp cloth. Continue until you are pleased with the way it looks, varying small and large stars. Practice with the silver and/or gold outliners, which come in a tube, on the white tile until you feel you can control the flow.

VARIATION

This bowl looks particularly good with water inside it up to the imagined water line with lit colored floating candles on the surface of the water. The base of the piece has been painted with two coats of turquoise glass paint, which heightens the effect of the water.

TECHNIQUES USED

❋ stenciling using glass paints
❋ using texturing gels
❋ using gold and silver outliners

THREE

With the outliner, outline all the stars you have stenciled in. Wipe away any errors gently using a damp cotton bud so as not to disturb the stenciling underneath. Allow at least 10 minutes for this to dry.

FOUR

Squeeze a walnut-sized piece of gold gel onto the tile. With the round-ended kitchen knife fill in the stars with the gel. Do not smooth the surface as the uneven finish of the gel catches the light when it is dry. Allow at least 24 hours for the gel to dry. You can then paint over the gel if you wish to deepen a color with the glass paints.

TEXTILES

Stenciling is a very effective way of adding regular pattern to fabrics. Plain fabric such as calico, with its natural cream tones, can be greatly enhanced with colorful stenciled designs to make charming cushion covers, drapes, tablecloths, tray cloths, bed covers, and many items of clothing: the possibilities are endless.

It is especially satisfying to be able to follow through a theme by coordinating a design and repeating motifs on drapes, cushions etc.

Blinds can be made interesting with the addition of simple stenciled motifs. As every type of fabric reacts differently to paint, it is advisable to try out your ideas on a test piece first before working on the finished piece and make sure that all surfaces are clean before you start working. As well as spray paints there are a number of fabric paints available which can be heat sealed with a hot iron. Read the manufacturer's instructions carefully before going ahead with the project. An alternative is to make your own fabric paint by mixing latex or acrylic paints with one of the water-based glaze mediums which are currently available, enabling you to create your own colors. This can also be heat sealed. This medium can also be mixed with bronze powders to give a rich and luxurious look to your work.

LEAF-PRINT
quilt
Project by Caroline Brown

Quilting stenciled fabric is very effective and gives a delightful appliqué effect. The leaf shapes of this stencil are very easy to cut out, and the quilt squares have been stenciled in a random way, letting the colors gently overlap. The squares are individually quilted before being joined together.

YOU WILL NEED

- mask and goggles
- 18-in. squares cream polycotton
- lining paper or newspaper
- repositional adhesive
- stencil (template page 128)
- spray paints in yellow, flame red, green, blue, and brown
- 20 x 4 oz. pieces of batting
- pins, safety pins, cream quilting thread, and needle
- beads (optional)
- 1 piece of polycotton sheeting for backing, about 84 x 68 in.
- 2 strips polycotton for binding the long edges, 88 x 6 in.
- 2 strips polycotton for binding the short edges, 68 x 6 in.
- extra wadding for edges (optional)

ONE

Wear a mask and goggles and work in a well-ventilated area. Lay a panel of the material on a flat surface covered with clean lining paper or newspaper. Apply the repositional adhesive to the reverse of the stencil and press firmly down onto the fabric. Lightly spray the stencil with yellow paint. Follow this with some red paint aimed at the center of the design. This will give a glowing coral color. To shade the edges use a little blue and green paint. Always hold a piece of folded paper in your other hand to help direct the spray. Remove the stencil and apply it to the next panel using more adhesive if necessary.

TWO

Lightly spray the center of the stencil with blue paint then spray the edges of the design with a little yellow and red.

THREE

Make a "sandwich" of a stenciled panel, a piece of batting, and a polycotton backing panel, with the batting in the middle.

FIVE

Assemble the quilt panels in a harmonious pattern. Pin the seams together and machine stitch into four strips of five panels each. Trim the seams to 1/3 in. Machine-stitch the strips together and trim the remaining seams. Press lightly on the right side.

FOUR

Pin the layers together with safety pins placed about 4 in. apart all over the design. Starting on one side quilt the layers together using a small back stitch or running stitch, making sure the stitches go right through to the back. (The quilting can also be machine-sewn.) Remove the safety pins as you work across the design. Sew on beads if required at this stage.

SIX

Lay the quilt on the piece of backing fabric. Knot the layers together in the center of all the interior seams, working from the top. Bind the edges of the quilt with the strips of backing fabric, machine-stitched onto the reverse side of the quilt and folded onto the right side. If you wish to add an extra strip of batting, fold this into the binding before stitching down firmly by hand. Bind the two long sides first, then the two short sides, butting up at the corners. If desired you can also sew on small bows for extra effect.

CORNUCOPIA
picture
Project by Caroline Brown

This stencil has been cut out in three parts. One for the greens, one for the reds and oranges, and one for the blues. This is to keep the colors separate when using spray paints. On a small design it is easy to get too much color overlap, which results in a dull and muddy effect. For register marks, used to position the stencil accurately, I have cut out two leaves on each of the red and blue stencils. These are covered with masking tape once the stencil is in position.

YOU WILL NEED

- mask and goggles
- 2 x 18-in. squares unbleached calico
- lining paper
- repositional adhesive
- stencils (template page 129)
- spray paints in green, blue, yellow, flame red, and a dark pinkish red
- masking tape
- 1 x 18-in. square, 2-oz. batting
- safety pins, cream quilting thread, and needle

ONE
Wear a mask and goggles and work in a well-ventilated area. Lay a piece of the material on a flat surface covered with clean paper. Apply repositional adhesive to the reverse side of the leaf stencil. Press the stencil firmly down onto the fabric.

TWO
Spray lightly with green paint shaded with red. Remove the stencil. Remember to hold a piece of folded paper in your other hand as you are spraying, to help direct the paint.

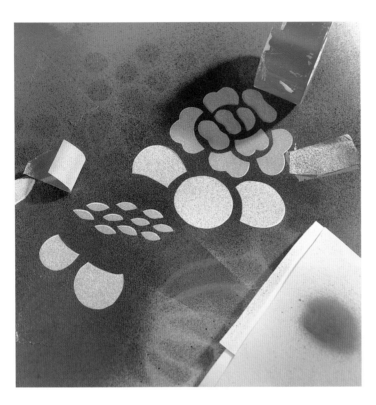

THREE

Use the leaf register marks as a guide to position the second stencil for the peaches and flowers. Once you have positioned the marks you should cover them with masking tape before you start to spray.

FOUR

Spray the peaches with yellow paint, shaded lightly with red. Spray red paint onto the flower and melon seeds. Remove the stencil.

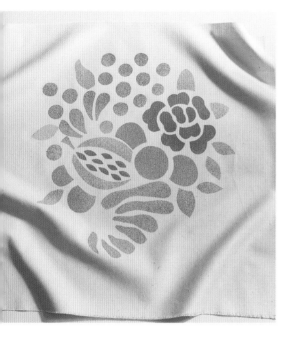

FIVE

Again using the leaf register marks as a guide and remembering to cover them with masking tape, apply the blue stencil (grapes and figs) to the fabric. Using the blue and dark pinkish red paint, spray the grapes and figs, adding more blue to the figs to make them darker. Remove stencil. Quilt the picture in the same way as shown on pages 62–63. To show the completed picture to good advantage, mount in a narrow, delicately colored wooden frame.

CLAYFIELDS
cat cushion
Project by Caroline Brown

The Clayfields Cat appeared on the scene some years ago, a tiny starving scrap of fur. She has grown into a sweet-tempered beauty of subversive charm and winning ways. Her tabby markings were the inspiration for this stencil.

YOU WILL NEED

- mask and goggles
- 2 x 20-in. squares unbleached calico
- lining paper
- repositional adhesive
- stencil (template page 130)
- masking tape
- paper towels
- spray paints in yellow, red, blue, green, and brown
- black waterproof pen
- cotton buds
- newspaper
- 1 x 20-in. square batting
- 2 pieces 20 x 14 in. calico for the back of the cushion
- pins, safety pins, red beads (optional)
- cream quilting thread and needle
- a piece of calico 6 yds x 5 in. for the frill
- cushion pad

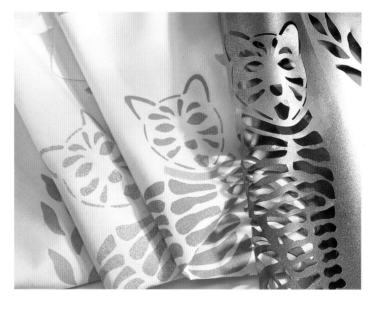

ONE

Wear a mask and goggles and work in a well-ventilated area. Lay a 20-in. square of fabric on a flat surface covered with clean paper. Apply repositional adhesive to the reverse of the stencil and press the stencil firmly onto the panel of fabric. Using a strip of masking tape cover the cat's collar. Cover the cat part of the stencil with paper towels, stuck down with masking tape. Hold a piece of folded paper in your other hand to help direct the spray.

Spray the leaves green adding random touches of red and yellow to give a mellow color. Remove the paper towels from the cat and mask off the leaves in the same way. Spray the cat with yellow paint, follow this with red, and finish with brown to shade the ears, tail, and back. Remove the masking tape from the cat's collar and spray this blue or another color of your choice. Mask round the collar before you spray.

TWO

Draw round the cat's features using the black waterproof pen to accentuate the eyes, nose, tongue, and whiskers.

FOUR

For the frill, fold the long strip of material in half lengthwise and pleat up neatly into a continuous frill. Machine-stitch ⅓ in. from the edge and press.

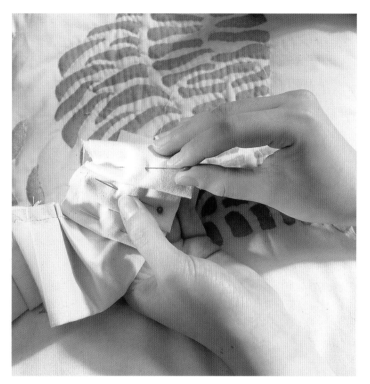

TECHNIQUES USED

❋ stenciling onto fabric; using aerosol paints to achieve color blends
❋ making a frilled cushion

THREE

To add the red berries spray a little of the red paint into the aerosol cap, dip in a cotton bud, and dot onto the fabric. Practice this on newspaper first, otherwise use a red waterproof pen. Quilt round the design as shown on pages 62–63, making a sandwich of the stenciled panel, batting, and backing and stitch through all the layers. Sew the red beads on top of the berries.

FIVE

Attach the frill to the front of the stenciled cushion panel, raw edges together, with the frill pointing inward. Machine-stitch in place. Where the ends of the frill meet, hand sew to make a neat join.

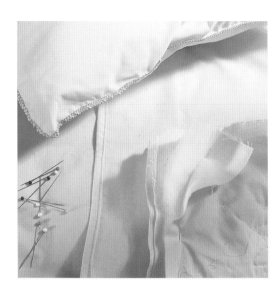

SIX

Make a 1-in. hem along one long side of each piece of the two pieces of calico for the cushion back. Overlap the hemmed edges by 3 in. to make an opening for the cushion pad. Machine-stitch in place. Lay the cushion back on top of the cushion front, right sides together. Pin in place and machine-stitch through all the layers. Trim the seams and turn cover to the right side. Iron the completed cover and insert the cushion pad.

PAISLEY
drapes

White cheesecloth drapes with the light streaming through are both practical and beautiful. Stenciling gives you the freedom to decorate them in any way you wish, perhaps to pick out existing patterns already in the room where they are to be hung. Cheesecloth also makes elegant bed drapes. The design can be stenciled all over or as a deep border with a narrow border as an edge, as demonstrated here. I love the effect of white on white, which gives an even more ethereal feel. I have used white fabric paint, which I have stenciled on with a miniroller. This is a quick and easy way of stenciling, provided the golden rule is maintained—use very little paint and build it up gradually.

YOU WILL NEED

- tape measure
- white cotton thread
- stainless steel pins
- scissors
- a length of cheesecloth allowing at least 10 in. to spare for hems, trimming, etc. and a spare piece for testing your design
- white fabric paint
- mini sponge roller and tray
- paper towels
- stencils (templates page 131)
- repositional low-tack adhesive

TECHNIQUES USED

❀ stenciling a length of fabric
❀ using fabric paint
❀ stenciling with a miniroller

ONE

Wash and iron the fabric first to remove the dressing put onto new material by the manufacturers. Make up the curtain allowing a 3-in. hem at the bottom and the heading you have decided on for the top. Iron out any creases in the material.

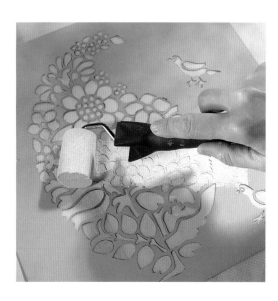

TWO

With a teaspoon, drop several spoonfuls of fabric paint into the well of the tray. Run the miniroller through this and work up and down the length of the tray to disperse the paint. Finally work the roller up and down onto paper towels until the paint comes out in a thin veil when tested. Test your design on a spare piece of fabric. Run the roller lightly to start with, increasing the pressure as you go; you will then find the paint does not come out too quickly.

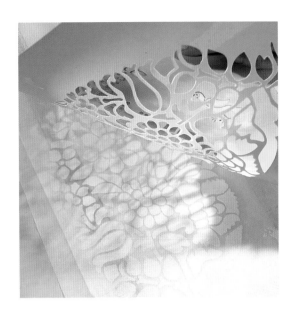

THREE

Pin the curtain onto the ironing board, slipping a paper towel underneath the area you plan to stencil. Having covered the back of the stencil in repositional low-tack adhesive, position the stencil using the hem as a guideline. If you are making two drapes, position the stencil so that there is a whole pattern against the leading edge of each drape. If only one drape is to be made start the stenciling at the center of the drape and work outward towards each edge. The pattern given for this project has two little birds on each side of the Paisley motif. These can be used as registration marks to make sure the Paisley motif is always evenly spaced.

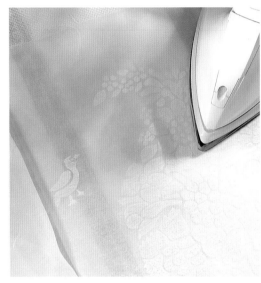

FOUR

When the stenciling is complete and the paint has dried turn the drape over and seal with a hot iron according to the manufacturer's instructions. There is a second narrow border given with this project which can be stenciled under the Paisley motif if required, using the same procedure and using the bottom of the second stencil to make sure that it is evenly spaced from the edge.

S O F T *toy*

The stencil for the soft toy will either make a little doll which can hang at the end of a baby's crib or it can be appliquéd onto a bag, the front motif on one side and the back on the other. A child's name could also be stenciled on the bag. Use only textile paint which is nontoxic.

YOU WILL NEED

- pencil
- craft knife
- scissors
- stencils (templates page 132)
- paper doily
- masking tape
- 1 20-in. length calico
- wooden board or ironing board for stretching the calico
- pins
- paper towels
- repositional adhesive
- nontoxic textile paint in bright blue, bright red, white, and black
- 3 stencil brushes
- white tile
- cotton bud
- iron-on interlining
- 1 5-in. thick foam sheet—62 in. square
- tacking thread
- needle
- cream and black thread

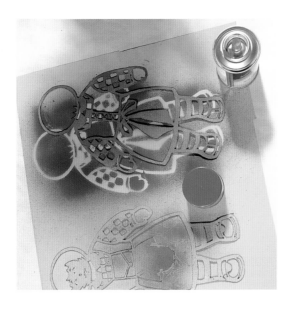

ONE

Wash and iron the calico first to remove any dressing. Trace stencil shapes and then draw a line around the whole stencil to create a narrow seam allowance around the edge. Carefully cut around this shape with a craft knife (before doing this refer to steps two and three). When you stencil, the paint will go over the edge of the doll shape and when this is lifted there will be a white line where the seam allowance is.

TWO

For an added decorative element you can add lace to the base of the apron by snipping off a small part of a paper doily.

FOUR
Stretch the calico firmly across a wooden board and pin it in place. Place a paper towel under the calico to soak up any excess paint. Run the repositional adhesive on the reverse of both the front and back stencils and fix in place on the calico.

THREE
Attach the doily frill to the base of the apron on the front stencil with a narrow strip of masking tape on both sides. Do this after you have cut out the stencil shapes but before you cut round the whole shape for the seam allowance. Remember to keep the hair shape that has been cut out, as it will be needed later.

FIVE
Stencil in the hair and shoes in black on the front and back of the doll.

SIX

Leaving the stencil in position, stencil in the pinafore dress in blue, stippling firmly through the lace. Stencil in the blouse and striped stockings in bright red on the front and back.

SEVEN

To stencil the face, remove the stencil of the front of the doll and lay the hair shape in place. Mix a small amount of the red and white textile paints on the tile, adding the red to the white a little at a time until a flesh color is produced. Stencil in the face with this, adding a small amount of red to color the cheeks. Remove the mask for the hair, and replace the stencil. Stencil the mouth and the nose in red and the whites of the eyes in white. The eyebrows are in black. Stencil the flesh color onto both of the hands, front and back. Remove the stencil and add the center of the eyes with a cotton bud dipped in blue paint.

EIGHT

When the paint has dried, remove the calico from the board and iron on the back to heat seal. Cover the back with an iron-on interlining. Draw the doll shape onto the foam sheet, using the stencil if necessary, and cut away the seam allowance around the foam shape. Cut the front and back sections of the doll on the seam allowance.

NINE

Tack the foam to the inside of the back section of the doll.

VARIATION

Although the instructions are for a doll with dark hair, different colors can be used but remember to change the color of thread according to the color of hair used. The stencil could be used round a child's room as a border and on a number of other items.

TEN

Take the front section of the doll and, carefully matching to the back, tack together making sure that the foam does not show. Using cream thread in the sewing machine stitch all around the doll with straight stitches 2.0 long. Turn the stitch length to 0 and the zigzag to 1.5 and zigzag all round the doll (apart from the hair) in the cream cotton. Zigzag across the base of the dress. Using a straight running stitch, stitch round the chin. Rethread the machine with black cotton and zigzag around the hair as before. If you do not have a sewing machine, sew securely by hand.

FURNITURE

It is when decorating furniture that stenciling really comes into its own. Here you have the possibility to retrieve and transform unloved but useful pieces of furniture. You can also find furniture in thrift shops, at auction sales or even by rescuing pieces that have been thrown away. It is, however, a good idea to look at the shape of the piece upon which you are about to spend some time and effort. If something is a really ungainly shape then all your efforts could be wasted.

Although suggestions have been given for painting furniture to be stenciled, very pleasing results can be achieved by working onto bare wood with the discreet addition of stencils in wood tones or folk designs in bright colors.

On the whole, provided the piece is in reasonable condition and depending on how much time you plan to spend on it, most items of furniture can be improved with a little thought and planning and, who knows, you may find yourself with a new decorative idea which is just right for that neglected piece of furniture which was so dull and unattractive that it had to be relegated to the attic or cellar.

HANGING
wall closet

The panels have been used to demonstrate how effective a textured finish can be. Each facet is decorated with bright and cheerful ice-cream colors, finishing with a cone in the center panel. To achieve a textured stencil a two-part stencil is used. The trellis panel of the ice-cream cone works particularly well with this technique. To achieve the ice-cream colors, use sample pots in strong colors such as shocking pink, lilac, pistachio green, all toned down with a lot of white.

YOU WILL NEED

- spray paint to make two-part stencil
- stencil (template page 133)
- low-tack masking tape
- tube acrylic paints in cadmium red for the cherry, mid gray, yellow ocher, burnt umber, titanium white
- 3 stencil brushes
- white tile
- cotton buds
- nonpermanent repositional glue
- small disposable pot to mix the textured paint
- a tube of ready-mixed filler
- spatula or flat-ended kitchen knife
- damp rag
- dead-flat acrylic varnish

ONE

The first stencil consists of a trellis design, swirls of ice-cream and a cherry. Make a second stencil by laying the first stencil on a fresh piece of stencil card and spraying through the design with spray paint. Cut out the whole shapes—cherry, two pieces of ice cream and the cone without the detailed design and keep the shapes you have cut out for masking. Lay the second stencil shape onto the panel. Fix in position with low-tack masking tape. To stencil the ice-cream, mask the cone with the cut-out cone section and stencil the ice-cream background in a mix of mid gray and titanium white acrylic paint. Remove the cone mask and, leaving the stencil in position, mask off the ice-cream section with the cut-out ice-cream section. Stencil the cone in a mixture of yellow ocher, burnt umber, and titanium white. Stencil the cherry in red. With a cotton bud remove a highlight on the cherry while the paint is still wet. Remove the stencil and allow to dry.

TWO

Cover the back of the first stencil lightly with nonpermanent repositional glue. This is important because, to be effective, the texture mix must not seep under the stencil. Lay the stencil over the already stenciled basic shape to make sure it matches exactly. Cover the cone base with the mask as before. Mix together the filler, a little yellow ocher, and titanium white in the plastic pot. Using the spatula work the mix over the ice-cream section as shown.

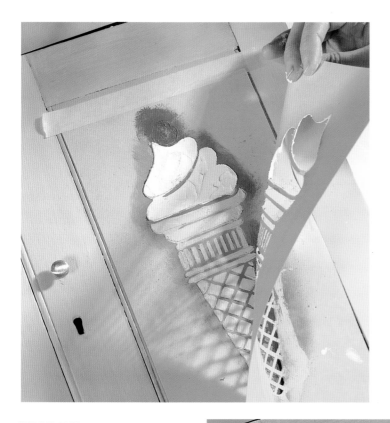

TECHNIQUES USED

❀ creating and using a two-part stencil
❀ working with filler to give a textured finish
❀ softening colors to give vibrant or ice-cream colors

THREE

Leaving the stencil in place, lightly mask off the section covered with the texture mixture. For the cone mix some yellow ocher, titanium white, a little burnt umber, and some filler and work this over the cone area. Carefully remove the stencil and wipe it down immediately with a damp rag. When the filler has completely set varnish over the entire panel with dead-flat acrylic varnish.

ARMOIRE

The old armoire used in this project was a wonderful find. Once it had been stripped of its many layers of paint the quality of the wood and the care with which it had been put together became obvious. As it had many molded panels on the front of the doors a design in Pennsylvania Dutch style seemed appropriate. I used traditional paints throughout because they give a mellow painted look to the work (although latex or emulsion paint could be used just as effectively). Traditional paint was also used for the stenciling. This paint dries very quickly, is easy to stencil with, and can be bought in small sample pots, which are perfect for stenciling. It does, however, need to be sealed at each stage with acrylic varnish but both the paint and the varnish dry extremely quickly.

YOU WILL NEED

To prepare the armoire:

- sandpaper
- sanding sealer
- wood filler
- 16 fl. oz. terracotta-colored paint
- 3 2-in. brushes
- 1 candle
- masking tape
- smaller amounts of pale yellow for the center panel, and dark blue/green for the surround
- fine wire wool
- dead-flat acrylic varnish
- stencil (template page 134)

To stencil the designs:

- lining paper
- non-permanent repositional glue
- 5 stencil brushes
- paint in deep yellow, deep red, charcoal, green, and white
- a white tile to use as a palette for the paint
- cotton buds
- paper towels
- clear wax
- soft cloth (an old T-shirt is ideal), cut into squares

ONE

Sand all over to provide a key for the paint. If the wood is new, seal with sanding sealer. Fill any holes or cracks with wood filler, and sand down. Paint the whole surface of the wood with terracotta paint and allow to dry. Using the candle, rub firmly over areas where there would have been wear—along corners, around any keyholes, and occasionally in the center of the panels.

TWO

Mask around the outside edge of the molding with masking tape. Do this just before you begin to paint: masking tape can be difficult to remove if left for 4 hours or longer.

THREE

Paint the whole armoire, except for the panels, with the dark blue/green paint.

SIX

Rub over the entire armoire with fine wire wool paying special attention to the areas where the candle wax had been applied. The base color will be revealed here and there. If you feel you have removed too much of the second color, you can paint those areas again.

FIVE

When the tape is removed, the moldings will be revealed in the terracotta base color.

SEVEN

When you are satisfied with the way the armoire looks apply one coat of dead-flat acrylic varnish all over. This will protect your work when you come to stencil and enable you to make corrections to the stenciling without the base coat being altered.

FOUR

Remove the masking tape and reapply around the inside of the molding and paint the panels pale yellow.

NINE

As there are so many panels, set out everything you will need in an organized way and establish a routine.

EIGHT

This armoire has different-sized panels so the stencil is repeated vertically for the larger motifs. Try this out on lining paper first. Position the stencil on the baseline and slide it up to fill the large empty space. If you feel daunted by the idea of stenciling on all those little black dots, just leave them out—they can be put on later.

TEN

Cover the back of the stencil with nonpermanent repositional glue. First paint the tulips in yellow and, leaving the stencil in place throughout, paint the tips and bases of the tulips in red together with the pot.

ELEVEN

Stencil all the stems and dots (unless you intend to add them later) and little birds in black together with the outer parts of the pot. Stencil in the leaves in green and go over the birds in white. Remove the stencil. Now paint in the black dots for the eyes of the birds and the dots around the design if you prefer this method to stenciling. Use a cotton bud dipped in black paint with the surplus wiped off on paper towels. When your work is quite dry you can rub over some of the stenciling with fine wire wool to give a worn appearance. Paint on a coat of dead-flat acrylic varnish to protect your work. Leave this to dry, and then to give it a mellow, aged look use a coat of good-quality clear wax, rub in well and leave to dry. Finally, buff with a soft cloth.

TECHNIQUES USED

* rubbing back and distressing the base coat
* using a wax resist
* simplifying the problem of having to pick out the moldings by using masking tape
* using traditional paints to give a period look
* using wax to give a patina—this works especially well with water-based paints which seem to soak up the wax so that it becomes part of the final coat of paint in spite of the layer of varnish

COFFEE
table

This small low table with a drawer at the side did not look very interesting at first; the shape was not at all elegant. It was intended for a living room and by adding a checkerboard it could fulfil two purposes—a games table as well as a coffee table. Having painted it black to look more formal, it immediately seemed less rustic in appearance and much more suitable for the room for which it was intended. Black on its own can seem very stark and flat so by painting on a layer of barn red underneath and lightly rubbing away the top layers at the corners to reveal the red, the whole piece becomes warmer and livelier. The Turkish design and the gold lining down the legs and round the edges adds interest and makes the table more suitable for formal use.

YOU WILL NEED

- sandpaper
- wood filler
- barn red emulsion or traditional paint
- 2 x 2-in. brushes
- high-gloss floor-quality acrylic varnish
- heavy-duty acrylic varnish
- black emulsion or traditional paint
- fine wire wool
- dead-flat acrylic varnish
- metal ruler (nonslip)
- a piece of white chalk
- stencils (templates pages 135–36)
- set square to ensure the corners of the checkerboard are square
- low-tack masking tape
- red gold varnish
- paper towels
- pewter-colored varnish
- mineral spirit
- permanent gold marker pen
- small sponge
- red undercoat paint
- small bowl or saucer for the paint to be used in sponging

ONE
First prepare the table for painting. Rub down well with sandpaper to give a key for the new paint. Fill cracks and holes with wood filler. Paint over the whole table in barn red paint. Leave to dry. Seal with a coat of heavy-duty acrylic varnish. Leave to dry. Paint over a coat of the black paint. When this has dried, using fine wire wool gently rub the corners and edges so the red base coat can just be seen. Varnish. Leave to dry.

TWO
Find the center of the table by marking the center of each side and drawing across to the opposite side with the white chalk. Where the two lines cross is the center.

THREE
The checkerboard stencil allows for a board of 24 x 24 in. square. Mark this out with chalk using a set square to mark out the corners as shown.

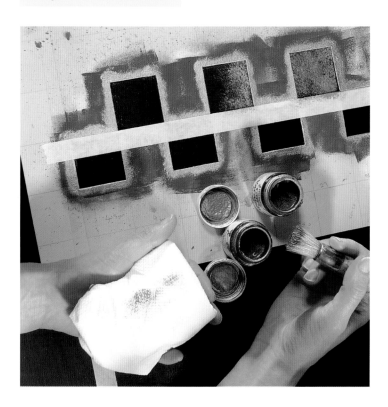

FIVE

Lay the stencil in position and run low-tack masking tape over the far edge of the squares on the second row. This will keep the edges crisp.

FOUR

Fix low-tack masking tape around the perimeter of the checkerboard area.

SIX

Shake the bottle of red gold varnish well. You will find when you open the bottle that there is enough varnish left in the lid of the container to use for the stenciling. Take up the varnish from the lid onto a clean stencil brush and wipe off the excess onto a paper towel. Using a dabbing motion so that the effect is slightly transparent, stencil the first row of squares. Remove the low-tack masking tape and tape across the far end of the first row. Stencil the second row in the same way. Continue across the board until you have finished stenciling all the red gold squares. Then, reversing the stencil, work all the pewter squares in the same way. Errors can be removed with mineral spirit.

SEVEN

Lift off the stencil and remove the masking tape. Using the gold pen and metal ruler draw a line around the edge of the board. Also draw lines across the checkerboard in each direction. Again, errors can be removed with mineral spirit.

EIGHT

Position the stencil intended for each end of the table, laying the center of the stencil on the chalk mark made to show the center of the table. Wet the sponge then squeeze out as much water as you can so that it is just damp. Dip the sponge into a bowl containing the red undercoat paint and gently sponge this across the stencil.

NINE

Leaving the stencil in place, sponge some of the red gold varnish across the pattern.

TEN

Stencil the other end of the table in the same way.

*A fruit-bowl design
in gold varnish would
also look effective on
the table.*

ELEVEN

Follow the same procedure to
stencil the pattern down each
of the long sides, matching
registration marks as you
work down the sides. Using
the gold marker fill in the
centers of the flowers, then
draw a line around the edge of
the top of the table. Turn the
table onto its side and draw
the lines round the edges of
the legs using the metal rule.
The pen's ink flows much
better if you use it on an
upright surface. Finally apply at
least three coats of high-gloss,
heavy-duty acrylic varnish.
Allow 2 hours for each coat
to dry. If you prefer, you could
stencil only one color on the
checkerboard, leaving the
background as the second
color. This is less labor-
intensive.

CHEST *of drawers*

This piece was already a pretty shape and I was fortunate in that it was made of medium-density fiberboard which had already been sprayed in white. This made an excellent base for a paint finish and I did not have to do any preparation work at all except wipe it down with a damp cloth and a little liquid detergent to degrease it. This is the only project in the book for which I used artist's oil paints. These are quite suitable for stenciling but they take a long time to dry and therefore need the addition of dryers. The same applies for alkyd paints. If you plan to turn the stencils over to obtain a mirror image as I have done here then you need two stencils, one facing the other, as the oil paint will not have dried and would leave paint marks on your work when you turn it over. You need to leave your finished work to dry for several days before varnishing with oil-based varnish.

YOU WILL NEED

- mid-yellow emulsion paint
- water-based glaze
- brush to apply the glaze
- tissue paper
- acrylic dead-flat varnish
- bright yellow, green/blue, raw umber, white oil paint
- white tile
- disposable plastic knife
- dryers (to speed up drying time of the oil paints; available from good art shops)
- mineral spirit
- brush for mixing
- stencils (press-outs provided)
- 3 stencil brushes
- lining paper
- paper towels
- disposable gloves
- polyurethane varnish
- lint-free rag

ONE
Label the position of the drawers with a marker inside so you know the order in which to put them back. Remove the drawers and, if possible, also the handles. The paint finish on this chest is frottage, so a glaze of half mid-yellow emulsion paint and half water-based glaze is used. Paint the glaze over the chest in sections, start with the top.

TWO
Lay crumpled tissue paper over the glaze and press down gently, then pull it away.

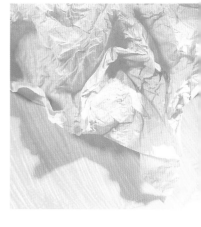

THREE
It leaves a soft marking as a base for the stenciling. Each section should be left to dry before going on to the next. When the glaze has dried paint a coat of acrylic dead-flat varnish over the whole chest, carcass, and drawers.

TECHNIQUES
USED

❋ frottage
❋ stenciling using oil paints
❋ using a stencil to fit round
   the drawers and top
❋ applying polyurethane
   varnish

FIVE

Having mixed your colors, test out your design on a piece of lining paper. Very little oil color is needed and the stencil brush should be well worked into the paper towel to remove any surplus paint before you start. Never at any stage of the work put your brush into the mineral spirit, as it will thin the paint so much that it will run under the stencils. Use two of each rose and flower stencils if you plan to reverse them.

FOUR

Decant the paints onto the tile using a disposable plastic knife for each color. Add a small amount of dryers to the tile. If necessary, thin paints a little with a few drops of mineral spirit. Mix the color of the bows and ribbons, adding the blue to the white and gradually adding a little of the yellow and then the raw umber to soften. Stencil the flowers in yellow, with white added, and the leaves in green with yellow added.

SIX

First stencil the whole shape with a thin film of color and then go over the areas like the center of the bow, the ends of the bows, and the ends of the flowers for a second time to deepen the colors in these areas. Replace the drawers.

SEVEN

Stencil the rose and ribbon design around the edge of the top of the chest and fill the center with the trellis design (template page 127). It is possible to see the shapes of the border through the trellis design and the stencils stop before overlapping the border. Stencil the bows on the drawers, just above the mark made where the handle was removed. The rose and ribbon design is made up by moving the stencils around to form a swag shape. Work out the combination on lining paper first. Reverse the design on the bottom drawer so that the bow comes under the handle, giving more balance to the design. Work the center of the rose stencil onto each handle. Leave the oil paint to dry for several days then, using the original glaze, define the moldings and area around the drawers by painting on two more coats of glaze, allowing drying time in between. Finally, apply two coats of polyurethane varnish, allowing drying time in between each coat, by the following method. Using protective gloves and a lint-free rag, dip the rag into the varnish and lightly wipe over the surface almost with a polishing motion. This avoids brush marks and gives a thin film, which dries quickly.

VARIATION

This project is a lengthy and time-consuming one. You may wish to omit some of the procedures, such as the frottage, or to use acrylic paints, that dry a lot more quickly, instead of oil paints. If you use acrylic paints, you would then use a water-based varnish as opposed to a polyurethane varnish. To simplify the project further, you could change the design, perhaps by omitting the trellis.

TOY BOX

This toy box was decorated for an 8-year-old boy. With its quaint soldiers standing guard, once again the source was colorful folk designs and I hope these timeless designs will give him pleasure for some years to come.

I was also able to include a number of decorative techniques in this project. Although I have described all the processes used in detail, you may wish to make your box simpler, leaving out some of the motifs or even enlarging some of them and using fewer stencils. You may not wish to texture the leaves and flowers, and instead just stencil the soldiers round the base.

YOU WILL NEED

- white acrylic primer, enough to paint the box
- 2 x 2-in. paintbrushes
- fine sandpaper
- sample pots of emulsion or latex paint in mid-yellow ocher, deep yellow ocher, and bright red, 8 fl. oz.
- a fairly stiff old brush, 3 in. wide
- dead-flat acrylic varnish
- flexible tape (useful to follow curves)
- acrylic scumble glaze
- easy-mask painter's tape 2½ in.
- low-tack masking tape
- white tile
- 4 stencil brushes
- paper towels
- stencils (templates page 137–38)
- repositional adhesive
- acrylic paints in deep green, ultramarine blue, titanium white, burnt sienna
- wire mesh (I have used a commercially produced copper texture sheet)
- paper doily or suitable length of lace for the tree stencil on top
- spray paint in deep red
- fine artist's brush for the unicorns' eyes
- floor-quality, water-based acrylic varnish

ONE

This box was made from medium-density fiberboard so the surfaces were already smooth. Remove the lid and retain the hinges and screws in a marked tin. Paint the whole of the outside with 2 coats of acrylic primer and rub down. To provide an interesting background for the stencils drag the lid and the whole box in mid-yellow ocher—mixing half-acrylic scumble glaze to half mid-yellow ocher paint. Paint the whole lid with the mixture. Taking the old stiff brush, brush firmly across the lid from side to side and you will find this leaves thin stripes of paint.

TWO

Set the lid aside to dry and repeat the process with the base, taking a side at a time. Leave to dry, and then paint over a coat of dead-flat acrylic varnish to protect the surface ready for stenciling. Run a line of easy-mask painter's tape around the top and base of the box. Place a line of low-tack masking tape along the inside of the easy-mask painter's tape and then remove the painter's tape. This will create the area for the border. Using the undiluted mid-yellow latex, paint the area for the border. Leave the paint to dry.

FOUR

To create another thin border fix two strips of tape with a narrow space between them inside the outer decorative border.

THREE

Put a teaspoon of deep yellow ocher paint onto the white tile, dip a stencil brush into this and work off the excess onto the paper towel. Having fixed the border stencil in place with low-tack tape, stencil working your way around the border you have painted. Miter the corners as shown in the section on cornering (see page 25). When dry, seal the borders with a coat of dead-flat acrylic varnish.

FIVE

Paint the space between the two pieces of tape red. If you have any moldings on your box they could be picked out in bright blue.

TECHNIQUES
USED

❋ two-part stencil using a
   negative stencil
❋ using textured plates under
   the stencil
❋ dragging
❋ using scumble glaze

SEVEN

Stencil in the flower shapes
using bright red.

SIX

To stencil the lid, position the
tree of life stencil in the
center of the lid using the
repositional adhesive on the
back and low-tack masking
tape to keep it in place. Stencil
the trunk first. Squeeze the
burnt sienna and ultramarine
blue onto the tile to make a
dark brown mix. Stencil in the
trunk and branches. Use a
mask to stop the paint
coloring the leaves and
flowers.

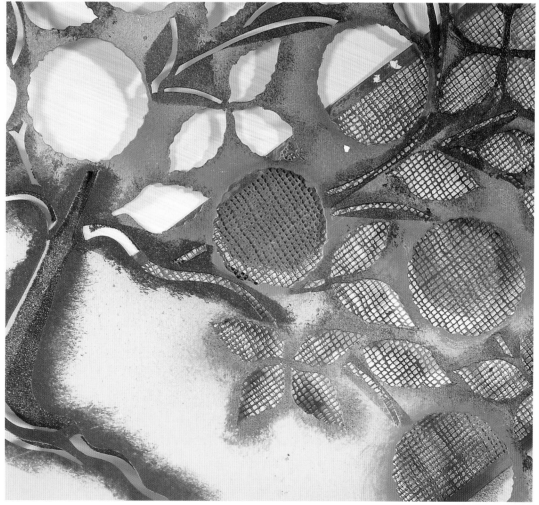

EIGHT

Slip the mesh texturing sheet
under the stencil; with the
dark green paint use the brush
in a stippling motion to stipple
through the leaf stencils,
remembering to use a guard
to prevent the paint from
going onto the flowers.

NINE

To add texture to the flowers,
find a suitable length of lace or
paper doily (you will need as
many pieces as there are
flowers), using the low-tack
masking tape, lightly tape these
behind the flowers. Refix the
stencil over the already
stenciled tree, mask out the
leaves and trunk, spray through
all the flower shapes (see page
26 for instructions on how to
stencil with spray paints). Fix
the soldier stencil in position
beside the tree making a mark
on the stencil to ensure that
when it is reversed to stencil
the other side, it is in the
same position. Stencil all the
red areas, the rosette in the
center of the hat, the trousers,
and cuffs. Leaving the stencil in
place and using a clean stencil
brush, stencil the coat in
ultramarine blue. Finally with
another clean brush using the
burnt sienna/ultramarine blue
mix, stencil the face, the
stockings, and the shoes. Add a
little more burnt sienna to
your stencil brush for the
musket. Stencil over the
stockings in white. Position the
small birds on each side of the
tree. Stencil initially in the
burnt sienna/ultramarine blue
mix, then with white paint.

TEN

Stencil the base of the box. Place the drum in the center of the front. The stencil for this is in two parts. First stencil the whole shape in the deep yellow ocher. Place the second shape over the yellow base and stipple in ultramarine blue (note that this is a negative stencil in which the background is cut away leaving the design so that when you stencil, the first color you painted will show the design). Arrange the unicorns on each side of the drum. Place the first unicorn in position. With the white paint stencil over the whole shape except the collar. Stencil the collar in red and the horn in yellow. With the burn sienna/ultramarine blue mix, add a little white and define the shape of the unicorn by stippling round the shape. Remove the stencil and add in the eyes and fill in the design on the collar with yellow. Reverse the stencil for the other side of the drum and follow the same procedure. Fill in the leaves around the drum using the texture stencil under the leaves. Stencil in the soldiers as already described. Reverse the blue and red coats of the soldiers on the front. Stencil a line of 3 soldiers along the side-ends of the box. To make sure that the soldiers are all the same distance from each other make a registration by cutting out a second musket behind the soldier so if you place the gun over the one on the previous stencil they will always be lined up. Screw the lid back into place. Varnish all decorated surfaces with floor-quality varnish, at least three coats.

VARIATION

As a finishing touch you could complete the box by painting the inside of the lid bright red and stenciling the child's initials in the center. This should be done before you fix the lid back into place.

FLOORS
& FLOOR-
CLOTHS

Rugs or floorcloths made of painted and stenciled canvas were first recorded in Britain in the 1720s and there are mentions of them being used in colonial America shortly afterward. Covered with many coats of paint and varnish, they were a decorative substitute for expensive rugs from the Orient. Sadly, few have survived because as they became worn, thrift prevailed and they were cut down to cover increasingly smaller areas, some eventually finding homes as book covers. They can be glimpsed as a background to many of the charming eighteenth- and nineteenth-century primitive portrait paintings in early America. Also, with modern decorating materials the problems of surface cracking is reduced. With the arrival of linoleum, floorcloths were used less and less. Today there is a revival of interest in these rugs and reproduced examples are often found in historic houses.

They are also enjoying a revival in the home because they are hard-wearing, needing only an occasional extra coat of varnish.

The earliest rugs were typically decorated with a checkerboard pattern. Later, designs following the patterns of Turkish carpets were used. In creating a painted floorcloth you have ample scope to give full rein to your imagination.

PAINTED *floorcloth*

The design I have used for this project was inspired by an advertisement for a beautiful wool rug in the Mogul style and although the pattern is not as intricate as the original, being formed of only three stencils and a border, it has translated well to the flat canvas.

Floorcloths such as this are best laid onto a hard floor, e.g., wood, tiles, or vinyl. If the floor is at all ridged several layers of newspaper can be used to act as a lining. As a safety measure fix into position with two-sided carpet tape or poster tack. Clean with a soft cloth or liquid detergent but do not scour or scrub.

YOU WILL NEED

For the canvas:
- a piece of heavy-duty canvas 4 in. larger all round than the finished size
- stapler/tack
- acrylic-based wood primer in white
- 2-in. decorator's brush or paint roller for the primer
- sandpaper
- craft knife
- scissors
- set square
- PVA adhesive
- spoon

To decorate the cloth:
- latex or emulsion paint in deep red, ultramarine blue, and yellow ocher
- 3 x 2-in. brushes
- 3 clean dishcloths or old T-shirts cut into large squares
- 1 in. masking tape
- low-tack masking tape
- stencils (templates page 139)
- acrylic paint in burnt sienna, ultramarine blue, titanium white, crimson red, and yellow ocher
- 4 stencil brushes
- white tile
- brush for mixing
- floor-quality acrylic varnish
- a brush or roller to apply varnish

ONE
Make sure your piece of canvas is large enough for the stencils you have chosen. Iron out any bad creases. Stretch the canvas to ensure a flat surface to paint on. Staple or tack round the edges making sure the cloth is taut. Cover with several coats of acrylic primer; allow to dry between coats. Lightly sand the last coat and remove any slubs with a craft knife. Remove the staples and trim the mat removing any uneven edges with the scissors. Check the corners with a set square. Make sure opposing sides are equal. Turn the canvas over onto its face, and turn over a hem of 1 in. all round, mitering the corners. Stick down with PVA glue, rubbing with the back of a spoon to make the hem lie flat.

TWO
Paint over the whole surface of the rug with a mixture of half yellow ocher latex paint or emulsion, and half water. While the paint is still wet dab at the surface with a clean dishcloth until you have an evenly mottled appearance. Leave this to dry.

THREE
Using the 1 in. masking tape, mask around the edge of the mat to the width of the planned border. Do this just before starting the next stage. Taking the second clean brush and dishcloth, paint the center of the rug using the deep red diluted with a little water. By painting the red over the yellow base a more interesting background can be built up rather than painting directly onto the white primer. Do not paint right up to the masking tape, or the paint may creep under it; instead use a dabbing motion with the dishcloth to bring the paint up to the masking tape. Again, dab over the surface with a dishcloth until evenly mottled. Leave to dry.

FOUR

Repeat the process around the area for the border using the third dishcloth and brush and using the ultramarine blue paint (diluted).

SIX

Using a clean brush, stencil the pale blue flowers with the ultramarine and white mixed on the white tile. Leaving the stencil in place mix yellow ocher and ultramarine blue to make green, and stencil the leaves with a clean brush. Deepen the tips of the flowers with a little blue.

FIVE

Remove the masking tape around the border, and clean up any paint which may have crept under the tape. Decide which of the flower motifs is to be the corner piece for the border. Using low-tack masking tape position the stencil in the first corner. Because the stencils are being worked on a rich background first stencil all the work with a light layer of titanium white. Do not remove the stencil. The white paint should dry quickly and will make the colors stenciled on top look far more luminous.

SEVEN

Stencil the flowers around the border in the same way. For the tulip-shaped flowers mix up a small amount of yellow ocher paint with crimson red and titanium white, and for the third group of flowers a little yellow ocher and titanium white. In each case deepen the tips of the flowers as you go along.

EIGHT

To work the yellow borders using the border stencil, work round just stenciling with burnt sienna. Because you are working on a pale background you do not need to underpaint the stencil in white first.

TECHNIQUES USED

❋ making a canvas floorcloth
❋ stretching canvas
❋ working out a border pattern and creating borders with masking tape

TEN

When the work has dried thoroughly coat with the floor-quality acrylic varnish. At least three coats of varnish are recommended. Allow two hours to dry. Allow four days for the varnish to cure before walking on the rug.

NINE

Register the border by placing the first flower over the last flower stenciled. Fill in the center of the mat, working across each clump of flowers in rotation. As mentioned earlier you should have calculated how many stencils go into the mat when cutting the size of the canvas at the start. between coats.

DECORATED *floor*

Decorated floors can be surprisingly hard-wearing and are an excellent substitute for rugs especially when stenciled across wooden floorboards. There are many design options to choose from: wood stains can be used to give the effect of inlay parquet, a checkerboard design in alternating colors can enlarge a room and look particularly good in a hall, marbled effects with classical borders can add grandeur or even a simple border running round a room can be effective. As long as the floor is in reasonably good condition the stencil design can be worked directly onto the floor. Stenciling provides an easy way of working a pattern across a large area.

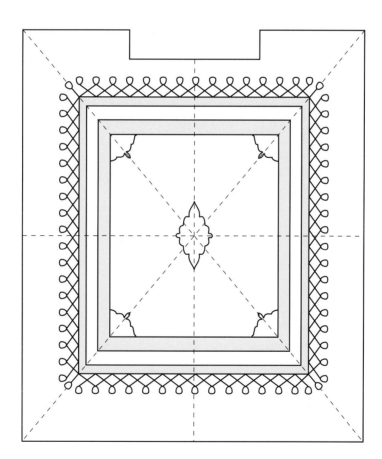

The design on the floor shown here was adapted from an antique Turkish rug, with richness built up by alternating broad and narrow borders. It is quite a time-consuming project as the design is so elaborate but the principles described remain the same even if you have something simpler in mind. Most paints suitable for stenciling work for floors. It is the varnish that keeps the paint fresh and in good condition. Because the floor has been sanded and previous finishes removed the paint sinks into the wood adding to its wearing properties. It is a good idea to store the stencils that have been used and to make a note of the paint colors so that minor repairs can be made over the years.

Before starting, a word of caution: when working on a hard floor such as this, always protect your knees by wearing knee pads or use a mat to kneel on. If working in a totally undecorated room paint the walls first, so that the paint does not drip onto your sanded unprotected floor. Clear the room of all furniture. Having first checked that the floor is sound, pull out all loose nails or hammer these below the surface then sand down the floor. Industrial sanding machines can be hired by the day. It is a good idea to make sure that the stencils you plan to use are on a large enough scale and are not likely to be dwarfed by the size of the floor. Scale them up with the help of a photocopier.

To mark out the floor (Figure 1), you need to find the center of the room and for this you need a chalk box. Ideally you need three people for this. The chalk box is filled

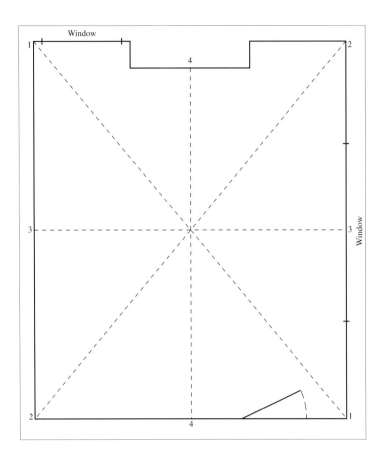

Figure 1

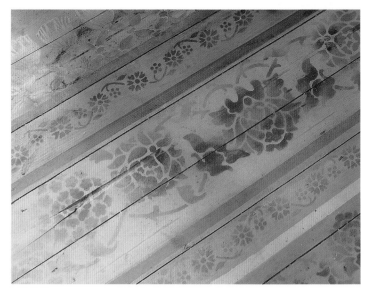

wash. When all the paint has dried, stencil first the borders then the central and corner areas. Mask over the central and corner motifs and stencil the all-over pattern across the main body of the square. When you have finished this remove all the tape. You can if you wish finish off with a tassel border around the whole square as was done here.

To protect your work use at least three coats of polyurethane matt varnish over the whole floor including the square, allowing at least 12 hours between coats. As maintenance, an occasional extra coat of varnish, perhaps once a year, may be necessary. To keep the floor clean, wipe over occasionally with a damp cloth.

with chalk and contains a long length of string; as you pull the string out of the box it will be covered with the chalk. One person stands at each of two opposing diagonal corners of the room holding the chalk-covered string just above the ground. The third person stands in what is approximately the center of the room, pulls the string upward and "pings" the string so that a mark is left by the chalk on the floor. Treat the opposing diagonals in the same way. Now make a mark at the center point of each wall, and mark a line across the room from center to center of each side (Figure 2).

Now decide the overall size of the area you wish to decorate and mark this out with decorator's tape, using your chalk marks as a guide to make sure that the square is in

the center of the room. Give the whole of the marked-out square a color wash of half emulsion/latex and half water, wiping off the surplus paint as you go to give an even finish. This forms the background. Leave it to dry. The photograph shows the sequence of borders used. Mark out the borders using masking tape (you may decide to use fewer borders than shown here). Do not leave the masking tape on too long or it will become difficult to remove. Alternate broad and narrow borders.

Give the borders outlined by the masking tape a second wash, using other colors as background for the stencil. Also give the central motif and corner pieces a second wash as shown here if you wish, leaving the main body of the square with just the original

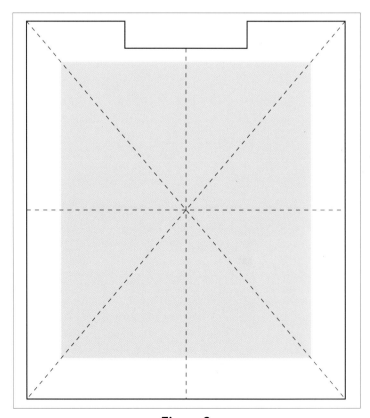

Figure 2

STENCILED ROOM

Stenciling can be used to improve and enhance a room. Ceilings can appear to be brought lower by painting a band of the ceiling color around the top of the room, reinforcing this with a stenciled border. A border can be stenciled at dado height, usually three feet from the floor, breaking up a large space of a wall and altering the visual proportions of a room still further.

For rooms with a very low ceiling, bands of a running border can be stenciled vertically in stripes from ceiling to floor.

Decorating a room can be a large undertaking so take time over the planning stage. An advantage with stenciling is that the work can be undertaken in stages. Try to make your work easier if you can. Stenciling a border above head height can be tiring on the arms, for example, and it helps to cut a second long border with several repeats so that you do not have to position your stencils so often and work therefore progresses faster. It helps to assemble everything you need in advance. A shelf attached to the top of your ladder to hold palette and stenciling equipment can save you running up and down. Protect the areas where you are not working with dust sheets and remove or cover any soft furnishings, which can be damaged with paints. A large apron with a large pocket in front to hold tape or chalk is helpful. Test the stencil colors against a sample board painted in the same color as the walls.

BATHROOM

This room is a family bathroom used by children so I wanted it to look fresh and fun. In order to give the whole room this fresh feel careful consideration was given to the colors. The images to be stenciled were inspired by marine imagery. Although the end result looks quite complex, only four stencils and two stencil borders were used.

The side of the tub was marked out in panels using masking tape and sponged across the tape in the same colors as those used for bathroom. This was varnished at the same time as the false tiles.

YOU WILL NEED

- 1 quart white latex/emulsion to match the ceiling and to paint the tiled area
- 4 quarts pale blue latex/emulsion
- 2-in. easy mask decorators' tape
- Stencils (press-outs supplied)
- plumb line
- poster tack
- chalk
- ruler
- sponge
- sample pots of pale orange, pale lime green, mid-blue/green, and terracotta paints, 8 fl. oz.
- 3 minirollers and trays
- paper towels
- fine line masking tape
- 6-in. ceramic tile
- 2-in. roller and tray
- heavy-duty high-gloss acrylic varnish

ONE
In order to make the ceiling look lower than it is, a border of the white latex ceiling paint was painted around the room to a depth of 10 in. The rest of the walls below this were painted in soft blue emulsion/latex, except for the area around the tub and behind the basin (where normally ceramic tiles would be placed) which was painted white. The skirting was painted blue to match the walls as were the architrave surrounding the doors and the panel along the side of the tub. Once the background paint had dried, a narrow border was stenciled just below where the white lowered ceiling and blue walls met. The color for this was the darker blue/green.

TWO
A large diamond pattern was then stenciled over all the wall areas painted blue. First the white painted areas which were to have the tiled effect were protected with decorator's tape. Using a stencil cut out to the shape of two diamonds next to each other, this was positioned below the border, which had just been stenciled around the top of the room. A plumb line was used. The string was suspended through the two vertical points of the diamond down to the skirting, having fixed the piece of string at the top with poster tack. A second plumb line was suspended in the same way through the second diamond. The line shown by the two pieces of string was marked with a piece of chalk down to the skirting using a long ruler.

TECHNIQUES USED

* ❀ changing appearance of a room's proportions with paints and stencils
* ❀ stenciling using minirollers
* ❀ marking out walls with a plumb line
* ❀ sponging through a stencil
* ❀ how to achieve a fake tile effect

THREE

The stenciling for this project is quick and easy. Dampen a sponge and squeeze out to remove all surplus moisture then dip into a saucer containing the lime green paint and sponge over the two diamond stencils. Move the stencil sideways and make a further two chalk marks in the same way, then sponge a diamond shape working all round the top of the room. The second row is quicker to do, as you only have to check your stencils against the chalk mark.

FIVE

To stencil the wave border around the area to be "tiled," run a line of fine masking tape around the edge of the area painted white. Using the wave border stencil as a marker, run a second line of fine masking tape along the bottom of the border. Paint the area in between lime green. Leaving the fine tape in place, stencil the wave border in mid blue/green, mitering as the corner is turned.

FOUR

Stencil the sea horses on every other blue space between the sponged diamonds. Put a few teaspoons of the pale orange emulsion/latex paint into a tray and run the miniroller through this. Run the roller several times across a pad of paper towels to remove excess paint. Having fixed the stencil in position, run the roller lightly across the design then, leaving the stencil in place, dip a clean stencil brush into the terracotta paint, remove the surplus onto paper towels, then stencil the edge of the sea horse to define the shape. Move the stencil across to the next blue diamond shape and continue the work. Stencil every other blue diamond until the row is complete. For the next row down, move the stencil across so the pattern of sea horses forms a diamond.

SIX

To create the tile look, mark off 6-in. squares using fine masking tape over all the area around the tub and behind the basin, having first protected the border just painted with decorator's tape. Use a 6 in. ceramic tile as a guide. Then, using a second miniroller and tray with the blue paint used on the walls, run the roller over the entire tiled area including the fine line masking tape, which should be left in position.

SEVEN

When the blue paint is dry mask every other square off with decorator's tape and, using a third roller and tray, paint over the squares that have been marked off with the lime green paint.

EIGHT

To stencil the fishes I used a pale orange emulsion and a miniroller. Place the stencil in position. Although there are only two fish stencils, I made these into a border as shown in the photograph using the tail of the first fish for registration, so that the pattern was always regularly repeated. Run the roller over all the fishes and then define the edges of all of the fish with a stencil brush and terracotta emulsion.

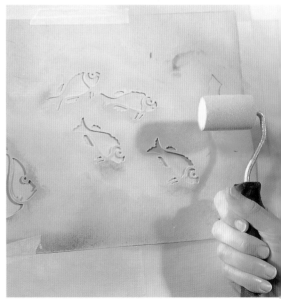

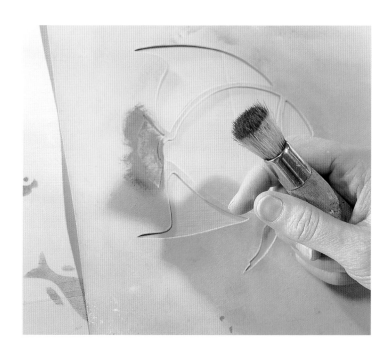

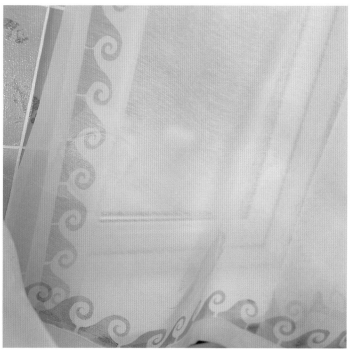

TEN
Stencil a coordinating border across the bottom of the curtain using fabric paints.

NINE
Move the stencil along using the tail as registration, as shown. When the stenciling is finished remove the fine line tape and carry out any touching up that may be necessary. With a 2-in. roller and tray and high-gloss heavy-duty acrylic varnish, apply three coats of varnish over the whole of the tiled area allowing at least two hours' drying time between each coat.

INSPIRATIONS

◀ Mirror frame in a damask pattern with spray paint. The striped or dragged background gives the effect of an antique fabric.

▲ This dividing door was stenciled with signwriter's paint. This paint is very suitable for glass—some varieties give a transparent effect similar to stained glass.

▲ Spray paints were used for this mirror surround, prettily decorated with blackberries and butterflies.

▲ A Victorian pine corner closet with the old varnish removed, stenciled with spray paint onto bare pine and waxed afterward with a good-quality wax.

▲ This tablecloth was decorated with the stencil used for the lampshade, which forms a half circle. The stencil design was reversed to form a full circle.

◄ This tray was stenciled with water-based wood stains which sink into wood to look like inlaid marquetry. The design can be outlined with a black permanent marker pen for further definition.

This tray was decorated with the stencil used for the jam jar covers, greatly enlarged. Acrylic paints were used. It was finished with a crackle-glaze in which a coat of water-based varnish was painted over an oil-based varnish. Because the water-based varnish dries quicker than the oil-based varnish it pulls apart as it dries leaving a cracked surface. Oil paint is rubbed into the cracks and when this has dried two coats of polyurethane varnish are painted over.

This stencil scene uses the technique shown in the bathroom project to create the effect of tiles. The radiator is decorated to match the floorcloth shown below it and a radiator cover cut and stenciled to resemble pillars. The inspiration for this room design came from Portuguese tiles.

◀ Items stenciled with ceramic paint.

◀ This bathroom was stenciled using spray paints on a ragged background, using imagery of doves, wisteria, and flower urns. The border around the basin was repeated with sand blasting onto glass shower doors.

These photographs show part of the drawing room from a large Victorian hall. Stenciling was set to suit the style and size of the room. To give the suggestion of embroidery onto silk, the panels had a thin glaze dragged or striped sideways, after the stenciling was finished, across each panel to reinforce this impression. The imagery was inspired by eighteenth-century Chinese hand embroidery.

TEMPLATES

Stenciling is about being able to create simple or complex patterns time and time again to great effect on a whole host of surfaces and items. In order to complete the projects in this book and achieve professional results, templates for all the stencils are supplied. Simply trace off, and follow the instructions on pages 19–23 if you need a little help. If the stencil is not shown as an outline, a press-out is included.

The press-outs are perfect for beginners who may be a little cautious about cutting out their own stencils.

The designs chosen are extremely versatile and can be used in many different ways. All you have to do is give some thought to the effect that you want to achieve and think carefully about the arrangement of the stencils and consideration to the background on which they are to be used. Experiment and practice and once you have mastered the basic techniques you can create interesting designs with professional results.

Lampshade

To trace at full size enlarge on a photocopier by 142%

Christmas Tablecloth

Garden Basket

Flower design for handle
included as press-out.

Tray

**Remaining stencils for this project
included as press-outs.**

Portable Writing Desk

**Remaining stencils
for this project
included as press-outs**

To trace at full size enlarge on a photocopier by 125%

Leaf-print Quilt

To trace at full size enlarge on a photocopier by 200%

Cornucopia Picture

To trace at full size enlarge on a photocopier by 142%

To trace at full size enlarge on a photocopier by 200%

Paisley motif/birds: to trace at full size enlarge on a photocopier by 178%

Soft Toy

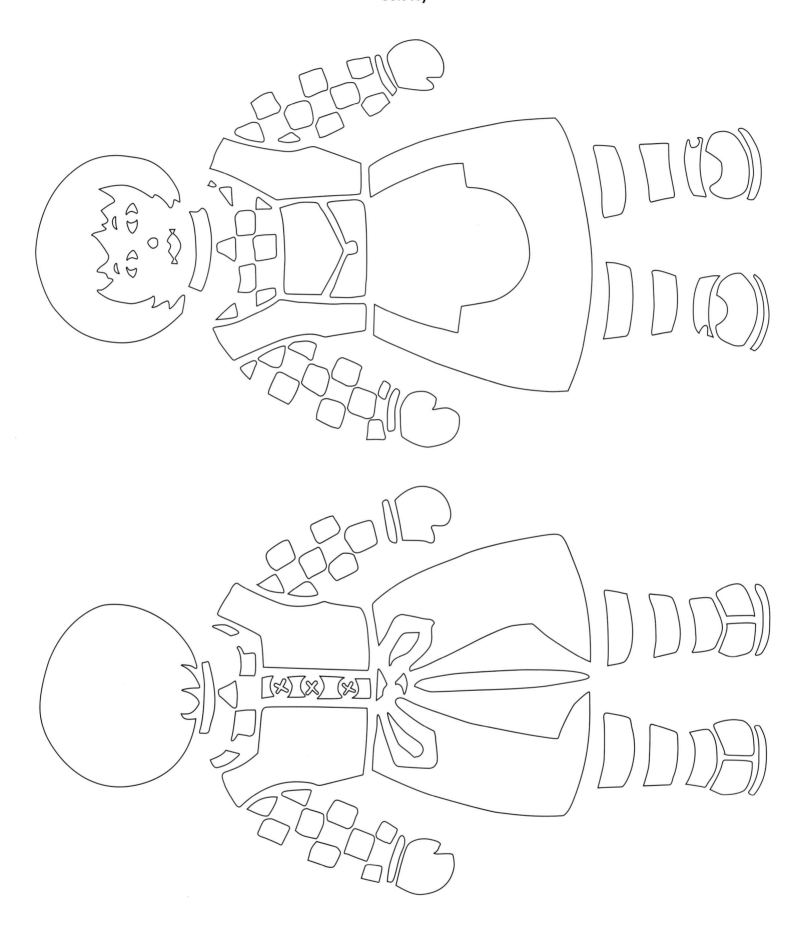

To trace at full size enlarge on a photocopier by 125%

Armoire

To trace at full size enlarge on a photocopier by 125%

Coffee Table

To trace at full size enlarge on a photocopier by 125%

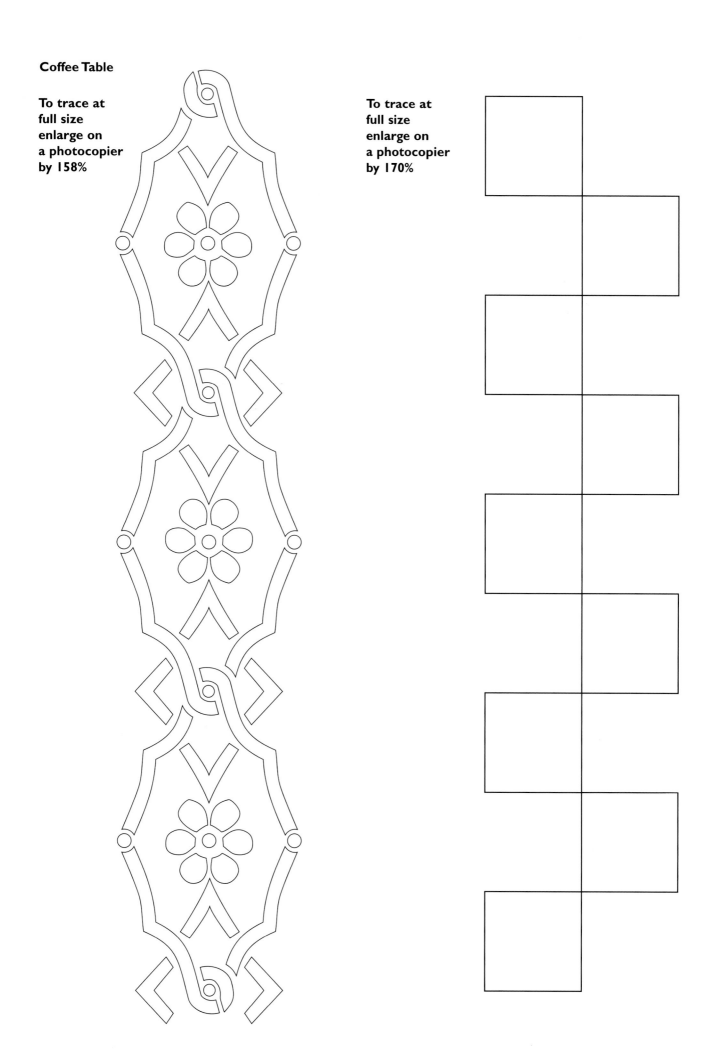

Coffee Table

To trace at full size enlarge on a photocopier by 158%

To trace at full size enlarge on a photocopier by 170%

Toy Box

To trace at
full size
enlarge on
a photocopier
by 277%

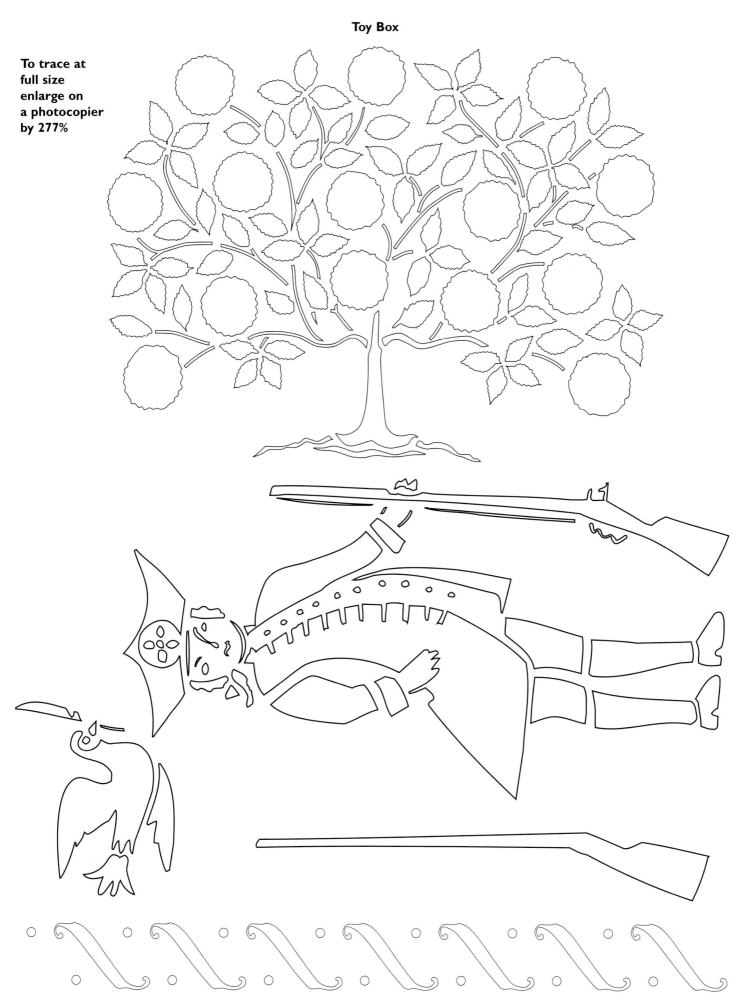

Border: To trace at full size enlarge on a photocopier by 220%

Toy Box

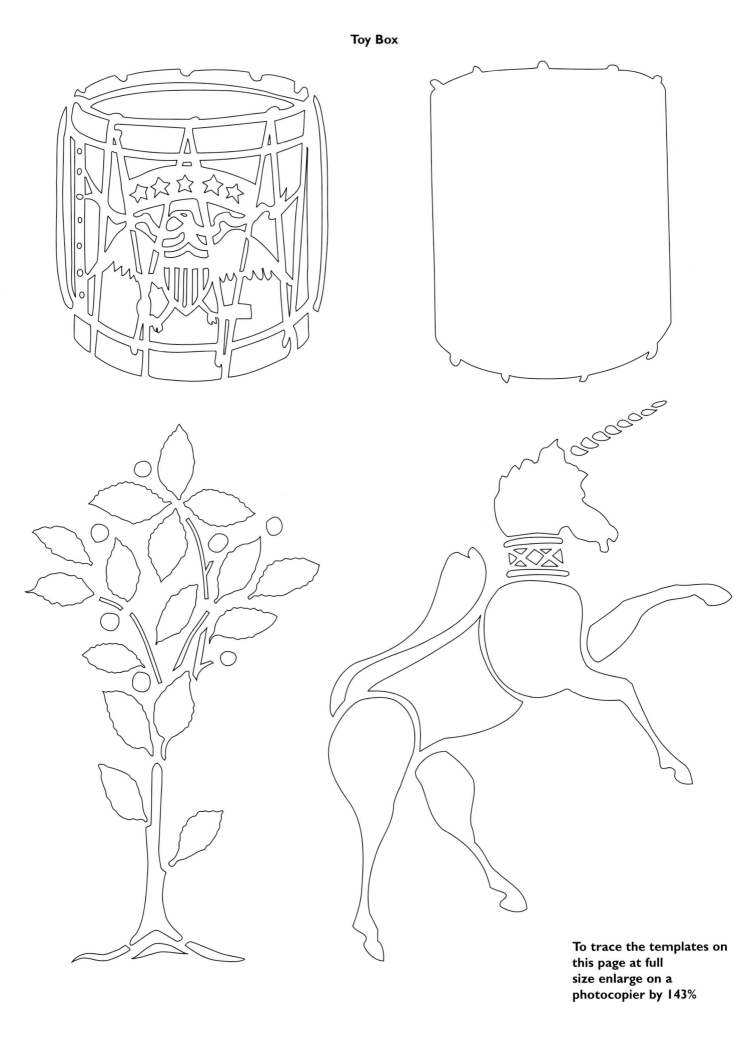

To trace the templates on
this page at full
size enlarge on a
photocopier by 143%

H

HALF-DROP term used in pattern making. A single pattern in its entirety is called a repeat. If a pattern is to be used to cover a whole area such as a wall it is usually repeated regularly by working the pattern at equal intervals from top to bottom, making a single patterned stripe. The next row down can either be made to match exactly the preceding one or the pattern can be started halfway down the pattern on the preceding row. This is called a half-drop repeat. The third row is the same as the first, and the fourth row the same as the second.

HEAT SEALING certain fabric paints can be made permanent and resistant to washing by sealing with a hot iron (on the reverse side of the painted fabric) at a temperature tested and recommended by the manufacturer.

HUE the description used to explain the actual color of something, e.g. variations of green—a blue green or a yellowish green. Sometimes it is possible to describe a color by referring to nature, e.g. sea green or leaf green.

I

IMAGE the likeness or representation of something. A mirror image is a likeness of a design in reverse, useful in pattern making.

K

KEY (in this context) to prepare a surface so that it can hold the paint. If the surface is very slick, e.g. a surface painted with gloss paint or a formica surface, it would need to be roughened with sandpaper in order for the paint to be able to grip.

KNOCKING BACK if a design is very bright and appears to 'jump' out of its background this can be irritating; this can be softened by gently dabbing a small amount of the background color over the design making it appear to blend in with the background.

L

LEAD PAINT any paint marked as containing lead is not suitable for painting items to be used by children or surfaces that children will come into contact with.

LIMING WAX modern liming wax is made from wax containing white pigment. Traditionally used on oak where the white goes into the grain of the wood to give a pleasing speckled appearance; can be used on other woods.

LINING here used to describe the making of fine lines to set off a piece of work, such as on boxes and pieces of furniture. Traditionally a technique used by coach painters, this was an exacting craft requiring practice. However a number of short cuts have been shown throughout this book which can be effective to frame and enhance a piece of stenciled work which do not require a lot of practice.

LINOLEUM hardwearing flooring manufactured from linseed oil, resins, and fillers.

LOW-TACK TAPE the best sort of tape to use when stenciling as it does not pull away the surface onto which it is stuck.

M

MANILA CARD oiled with linseed oil, it is the card traditionally used for making stencils.

MARKER PENS available in a variety of colors. The point can be thick or thin and the ink permanent or non-permanent in which case the work needs to be sealed. Very useful for filling in detail and making lines.

MARQUETRY decoration using veneers of different types of wood. Used on furniture and paneling.

MATTE a dead flat surface appearance which does not reflect the light or shine.

MEDIUM DENSITY FIBERBOARD (M.D.F.) board made of particles of wood fiber and a binding agent. Much in favor for furniture making and small objects previously made of natural wood. Protective masks should be worn when cutting or sanding M.D.F.

MINERAL SPIRIT used as a paint thinner and a degreasing agent.

MITERING a method of turning a corner when stenciling.

MOLDING an ornamental strip of wood which can be used as an edging e.g. around picture frames, as a dividing chair rail, on a wall, etc.

MYLAR a trade name for polyester plastic sheeting suitable for cutting stencils from.

N

NEGATIVE STENCIL the background of the stencil is cut away leaving the design uncut.

P

PAINT FINISH describes the various ways of distressing the surface of a painted area by covering the base coat with a wash, made up of either paint and water or paint and glaze, and while the wash is still wet, texturing or patterning the surface so that it comes away in areas to reveal the base coat.

PAINTS

Acrylic made by dispersing color pigment in acrylic resins, water soluble.

Alkyd paints made from synthetic resins. Have many of the properties of oil paints but dry quicker because they contain a drying oil.

Binders the materials used to hold the paint pigment to the base medium.

Ceramic paints some are solvent based and fired at high temperatures to sink into the surface glaze. For stenciling, water soluble paints can be used, which can be cured in a domestic oven.

Emulsion or latex water soluble paints used frequently for home decoration and are suitable for stenciling. These paints dry quickly and sample pots are usually available from hardware stores.

Fabric paints suitable for decorating on fabric. Follow manufacturers instructions.

Glass paints water-soluble paints are available which cure to enamel hardness and are suitable for stenciling.

Japan paints pigment ground in oil free resin varnish. Very quick drying. Excellent for stenciling.

Nontoxic paints these should always be used when painting items or surfaces that children will come into contact with.

Oil paints can be used for stenciling although slow drying times can present problems.

Signwriters' paints similar in style to Japan paints, although not as fine.

Spray paints available in a wide variety of colors, can be used to great effect, particularly to achieve subtle color blends.

Traditional paints give a chalky finish compatible with a period look.

PALETTE a surface such as a ceramic tile to hold the colors to be used in a project or a complete range of colors.

PAPER

Carbon used to make copies. Useful for transferring a design onto stencil card.

Cartridge the coarser grades of drawing paper.

Graph marked out with grid lines. Useful for designing patterns.

Graphite thin paper coated on one side with graphite for transferring designs. Marks easily erasable.

Lining paper used in household decorating for underlining wallpaper. Is a cheap paper to use for sketching and testing designs.

Tracing transparent paper used to reproduce a design.

PENNSYLVANIA DUTCH folk designs of German origin (when used as descriptive design term).

PERIOD LOOK incorporates the design characteristics of a certain period or time in history.

PINKING SHEARS scissors with a serrated edge which can be used to stop material fraying or to give a decorated edge.

PLUMB LINE or BOB a length of string with a weight on the end to check on the straightness of a vertical line.

POSITIVE STENCIL the design is cut out from the stencil plate and paint passed through the holes created onto the surface to be decorated.

P.V.A. (POLYVINYL ACETATE) a clear, white synthetic resin used in glues and for mixing with bronze powders etc.

R

RAGGING a paint finish where a contrasting glaze is painted over a base coat and the glaze, while still wet, manipulated with a rag to leave random marking.

REGISTRATION MARK a mark cut onto a stencil plate which helps with repeating the design.

REPEATED BORDER a border made by repeating the same design regularly, using registration marks.

REPOSITIONAL ADHESIVE makes the back of the stencil tacky so that it will adhere to the surface to be decorated and prevent the paint creeping underneath.

RESIST painting certain areas with a material that paint will not adhere to, so that when the work is finished it can be sanded and the paint will come away in those areas. Used in *Antiquing* and *Distressing*.

ROLLERS made of foam, those useful for stenciling are the 2 in. and 6 in.

RUBBING BACK an antiquing technique where several layers of paint, often of different colors, are sanded down to show the layers of previous colors to simulate wear.

RUNNING BORDER a decorated border formed of a repeating pattern.

S

SAMPLE BOARD a board painted with the colors and design that are to be used for a piece of work.

SCUMBLE a thin layer of transparent medium

containing pigment which can be used as a glaze over a base coat. Glazes can either be oil or acrylic based.

SET SQUARE geometric device used to check that a corner is square.

SOLVENT used to dissolve resins in certain paints and varnishes. Can be flammable and fumes can be noxious. Should be treated with care and manufacturers' instructions should be followed.

SPIRIT LEVEL a measuring device to check that horizontal measurements are aligned.

SPONGING a paint finish using a marine sponge to make textural marks.

STAY WET PALETTE commercially produced to keep acrylic paints moist.

STENCIL drawing or printing plate with parts cut out to form a design that is copied onto a surface and paint applied over the cut-out parts.

STIPPLING a paint finish made by tapping or pouncing a stiff brush over a surface, giving the appearance of orange peel.

T

TAILORS' CHALK used for marking fabrics, can be dusted away after use.

TAPE

Decorators paper tape that is adhesive along one edge.

Fine line used by signwriters to mark very fine lines.

Low-tack does not adhere too strongly, so is ideal to hold stencils in position.

Masking versatile, so is widely used in decorative painting.

Signwriter's low-tack tape available in various widths used by signwriters.

Stretch can be worked to go around curved surfaces.

Two-sided used for securing carpets or mats to the floor.

TEMPLATE pattern used as a guide for making designs.

TEXTURING imprinting a flat surface to give a raised or textured appearance.

THEROM STENCILING stencil without bridges so that the work looks hand painted.

TIFFANY GLASS Art Nouveau period glass decorated with abstract patterns and organic forms in iridescent colors.

TONE the range of shades within a color going from light to dark.

TOXIC a poisonous or harmful substance.

TRANSLUCENT allows light to shine through.

V

VARNISH transparent film painted over a finished piece of work that dries to a hard finish to protect it. Can be either gloss, satin, matte, or dead flat which reflects no light at all. Can be either solvent based, removed with white spirit, or water-based containing acrylics. The higher the gloss the harder the finish.

W

WAX good quality furniture wax can be used for finishing. Dark stained wax can be used to give an antique appearance. Blobs of wax can also be used as a resist.

WOOD PRIMER used to prime bare wood so that subsequent coats of paint will adhere.

WOOD STAIN can be found in colors to simulate a large variety of woods and are now made with an acrylic water-solvent base.

Christmas Tablecloth/Candle Holder

Christmas Tablecloth

Tray/Ceramic Jug

Picture Frame

Bathroom